Pools of Memory

The Sixty Year Odyssey of a
Devoted Fly Fisherman

Charlie Kroll

Frank Amato

PORTLAND

For Julia—
The best catch of all

"The last point of all the inward gifts that doth belong to an angler is memory. . ."
— *The Arte of Angling,* 1577

About the Author

Charlie Kroll was born and raised in northern Idaho where his father and grandfather were lumbermen. His early training favored hunting, fishing and biology. He obtained a B.S. degree in Zoology from the University of Idaho, took graduate work in freshwater fisheries at the University of Washington and worked as a field biologist in Alaska for three years.

After three years overseas as an army engineer unit commander during World War II, followed by his final two years of schooling, he went to work for the Bear Archery Company.

He worked for Bear thirty years, with one intervening period of five years during which time he traveled around the world, then worked as publications director and edited a national magazine for a Colorado-based sportsmen's organization.

He then returned to Bear Archery's advertising department to work on special projects, mainly writing assignments. He has authored three books and has hundreds of feature articles to his credit involving angling, bowhunting and wildlife.

He retired in 1988 at the age of 70, but continues to do freelance writing and to pursue the angling muse.

Published in 1994 by Frank Amato Publications, Inc.
P.O. Box 82112, Portland, Oregon 97282
ISBN: 1-878175-88-2
UPC: 0-66066-00174-0
Book Design: Charlie Clifford
Printed in Hong Kong
1 3 5 7 9 10 8 6 4 2

Contents

Foreword

Fly fishing is a world within a world and I was fortunate enough to have stumbled through its looking glass early in life.

It is an experience beyond catching fish, embodying relaxation, contemplation and the atavistic pleasure that comes with immersion in the natural world from whence we evolved. The process results in many perfect, isolated moments when time stands still and the artificial world of men dissolves in the mists of pure beauty and unhurried grace. He who has not explored for trout along the reaches of a wild mountain stream has not lived a full life, for it is in such places that a man finds serenity and fulfillment.

I want to quickly establish that this is not a "how-to" book. I assume my readers already know how and there are enough thoroughly detailed books available about all phases of the subject. Rather, it is an attempt to relive the interesting highlights of a lifetime of angling adventures—some still attainable, others not.

To many, fishing denotes a mindless pursuit for lazy people and conjures up the calendar vision of a barefoot, straw-hatted country lad asleep on the stream bank while his propped-up cane pole and dancing bobber go unheeded. In Walton's "contemplative sport" of fly fishing nothing could be further from the truth. It takes a lot of thought and a lot of physical exercise. If one had to work as hard at his job as he does during an average day's angling he'd be tempted to quit and go on welfare.

I like to keep my fly fishing as uncomplicated and unsophisticated as possible. It's a lot more fun that way. For those who want to memorize the Latin names of all the aquatic insect species and delve into the intricacies of hydraulics and limnology—more power to 'em. I'm happier when I put as little complication as possible between me and fooling the fish or vice versa.

As for those who argue against sport fishing on the basis of morality I am of the opinion they are badly mistaken. Fish from clean waters are one of the finest natural and healthful foods on our planet but to eat them we must first catch and kill them. The moral issue here lies in making good use of those we do kill and the proper care of those we do not.

In my experience, there appear to be six stages or plateaus of desire in the life of a fly fisher: 1) to catch a fish; 2) to catch a lot of fish (the limit); 3) to catch big fish; 4) to catch difficult fish under difficult conditions; 5) refinement of tackle and method; and 6) to catch a fish.

I make no apologies for the fish I've kept and still keep. Since early boyhood these numbers have never been excessive and one of the joys of my existence has been meals of fresh trout. I raised two youngsters and a wife on venison, grouse and brook trout and I believe they turned out none the worse for the experience. Crisp bacon and hash-browned potatoes with bannock and brookies cooked over the coals of a campfire is, for me, the ultimate gourmet meal, just add hot lumberjack-strength coffee or black tea. If at lunch or supper time rather than breakfast, a few baked beans laced with ripe olives adds a good touch.

I dislike reading stories that begin by describing favorite pools or stretches of water, yet coyly fail to mention the location (state, county or locale). It's not that I have to know how to get there so I can immediately rush out and flail the water to foam. Rather, it's a lack of personal involvement with the author's tale, a sense of being left out of the adventure, or at best viewing it through a glass darkly. I've tried to avoid that herein.

A quality angling experience does not have to include trophy-sized fish or completely pristine surroundings although the latter is often a part of it. Viscount Grey of Falloden said: "Thus as the angler looks back he thinks less of individual captures and days than of the scenes in which he fished."

Residing as I presently do, hundreds of miles from the nearest trout stream, I cannot fish every day as I did for years while living on the banks of Michigan's AuSable River. Southern "hawgs" and "bucket mouth" bass just don't do it for me. Saltwater fly fishing is fun but it's costly. You either have to spend a few thousand dollars on a sea-going boat, equivalent motor, trailer, hauling vehicle, etc., etc. or pay someone $350 or $400 a day to take you out. Instead, my personal preference is to spend what I can afford on annual excursions to trout or salmon habitat.

Like Mark Twain, when I was younger I could remember anything, whether it happened or not, but the time must come to all of us who live long when memory is more than prospect. Advancing years have now begun to limit my angling explorations but I live through remembrances that fill whatever time afield is lost.

The beauty of the waters I have fished for trout and salmon has given me a host of wonderful memories. Certainly these encompass much more than the rivers or streams, their forested or meadowed banks and the finny denizens that dwell there. Details drift in of the cries of loons, ravens and wild geese the enraged challenge of a bull elk, of the delights of a free-soaring hawk, flower-sprinkled alpine glades, sunrise gilding granite peaks, a mountain ram silhouetted on a crag, a water ouzel fearlessly plunging into the torrent, the webs of orb spiders jeweled with dew, fleecy clouds of midsummer, golden quakies among dark green ponderosas or a fawn curled up under the bracken. I can smell freshly cut western cedar, bacon frying and coffee simmering over a sage campfire, and see delicate brook primrose and shooting stars around a clear rill. I can taste freshly caught brookies or cutthroats, sourdough pancakes dotted with huckleberries and a day's-end libation of Yukon Jack added to a tin cup of spring water.

I'm now getting to the point where I can't remember anything but I have a lot of great memories. A good share of this anomaly is due to a lifetime habit of day-to-day trip recording in a small notebook and of taking endless photographs. It's wonderful how looking through those past notes and photos can trigger instant recall of details otherwise long forgotten. Without my mini-library of field notes some of the inclusions in this book would not be possible.

This is a loose collection of tales rather than a single prolonged excursion; it can be wandered through as the spirit moves you. In other words, this book is calculated to provoke your own memories of these or of similar places and encounters.

Finally, before we begin, I'd like to set the stage with a quote from that great angling author, Henry Van Dyke: "There is no combination of stars in the firmament by which you can forecast the piscatorial future. When you go a-fishing you just take your chances; you offer yourself as a candidate for anything that may be going; you try your luck."

Now, let's try our luck.

—*Charlie Kroll*

Chapter 1

POOLS OF MEMORY

The Flume Pool

My paternal grandfather, William Kroll, was one of the old-time logger barons. During the 19th century heyday of those north-woods entrepreneurs, he built mills and established a private empire among the virgin white pine stands of Michigan's Upper Peninsula.

Shortly after the beginning of this century, when most of the giant pines had been harvested, he was one of the first to move to the untapped forests of the Northwest, building what was at that time the largest sawmill in the region at St. Maries, Idaho. Beginning in 1914, the mill and the town it spawned grew together in what was then fairly isolated wilderness. Both were on the banks of the St. Joe River, a sizable waterway fed by numerous mountain tributaries. The St. Joe flows into Lake Couer d'Alene some 15 miles downstream. Because of its heavily forested banks local residents usually referred to it as the "Shadowy Old St. Joe."

Logging operations were largely upriver from the mill, around the smaller outpost camps at Calder, Avery and St. Joe. Not only were annual log drives held on the main river but portions of several streams were diverted into huge V flumes that carried the logs at freight-train speed for miles, dumping them into the main stream adjacent to the mill. There they were held in large booms until being fed through the green pond to the ever-hungry saws.

The loggers, particularly the river drivers, were a tough breed. Mostly Scandinavians and French Canadians, they worked 14 hours a day and still found time for bunkhouse brawls and other diversions. One of these was reckless wagering on who could sink his boot caulks into a big log and ride it, standing, down the final mile of the main flume. None that I knew of made it all the way and for more than one it was the last ride he ever took.

The largest flume, some 10 miles in length, ended 10 to 12 feet above the river surface and the force of the water flow from it formed a deep and highly oxygenated pool. The natural mouth of the partially diverted stream nearby added additional current, oxygen and displaced aquatic insect life. The Flume Pool was a favored lie for a host of native cutthroat trout.

The St. Joe River was one of the finest cutthroat habitats in the West. Many races or subspecies of this excellent game fish

Mother beside the big flume that brought logs down to the St. Joe.

existed throughout the Rockies, from Alaska to California. The cutthroat had the largest original range of any North American native trout. They derived their name from twin slashes of orange-red on the underside of their lower jaw. Overall coloring varied with the regional strains. Those of the St. Joe are dark olive on the back with cadmium-colored sides fading to very pale yellow on the underside. They are quite heavily spotted with black, particularly over the rear third of the body. As table fare they are among the best of fresh water fishes.

My father had worked for his father since the age of 14, first as a logger then as mill store clerk and finally as the company comptroller. Having spent his life in and around the woods, he loved to hunt and fish. Mother, having also been born and raised in northern Michigan, enjoyed fishing even more than he did. I came by my love of the sport quite naturally. From the time I was old enough to hold a rod (six or seven) they took me with them on frequent outings up and down the river. Fishing spots were often reached with a light, strake-sided rowboat. Dad would anchor the boat in a position where I could fish from the stern, while he and mother cast from various spots along the river banks.

The tackle consisted of Bristol metal telescoping rods, light wire-frame reels, enameled silk lines, silkworm gut leaders and Indiana or Willow Leaf spinners baited with angleworms or grasshoppers, although dad often fished with snelled wet flies, using a tail fly and two or three droppers on his leader. His favorite patterns were the Mosquito, Western Bee, Red Ibis, Grizzly King, Montreal and Black Gnat.

The cutthroat were not too difficult to catch. The river was heavily populated and competition for food usually resulted in plenty of "takers." When time was a factor, good fishing was nearby. Our home was by the river near the green pond and adjacent rafts of logs. Dad had fitted a pair of mother's high button shoes with logging caulks with which she fearlessly walked the log booms to get within reach of good fishing spots.

On my eighth Christmas, Santa presented me with my first fly fishing outfit; an eight foot Horrocks lbbotson bamboo rod, a Martin automatic reel, silk enameled line and a leather wallet with a dozen or so snelled flies of various patterns. Right then and there I graduated from a pole fisherman to a fly angler, although admittedly in later years I often backslid, fishing with bait when brushy stream conditions necessitated it.

Mother fearlessly walked the log booms to reach the best fishing spots.

10

Contrary to what one might assume I was not taught fly casting by my father. He believed firmly in a boy doing things for himself. He saw to it that I had tackle; the rest was left up to me.

There were no instructional books on the subject, at least none that I knew of. I was self-taught, learning through trial and error the procedure that felt most natural and produced the best results. It seemed to come naturally and I didn't think much about the mechanics of it until many years later when I had the opportunity to assist Lee and Joan Wulff in their Garcia Fly Fishing School on Colorado's Elk River.

Not being happy with the way silkworm gut leaders kinked and curled, even when presoaked between wet felt pads, I experimented for a time with horsehair leaders. I took a few dozen hairs from the long tail of a white horse that pulled the local milk delivery wagon. The leader was made up of three individual hairs twisted together for the butt section, knotted together with two strands for the midsection and one for the tippet. Total length was a bit over six feet. I coated the knots with clear lacquer, the same dope I later used to waterproof the heads of home-tied flies. I carried several extra strands curled up in my shirt pocket for tippet replacements. This occurred frequently for although these leaders were surprisingly strong in landing fish, underwater snags quickly destroyed them.

The St. Joe cutthroats ranged from one to three pounds (with a five pound fish being unusual) and were excellent fighters. When hooked they waged an underwater battle with a strong bulldogging resistance much like that of Eastern brook trout. I found later that they also rose well to dry flies but in my younger days the floating fly in that area was little-known and seldom used.

One of the most reliable places on the entire river was the Flume Pool. When logs were not coming off the flume, it could be depended on for a brace or two of 15 to 20 inch fish. It was there I had my very first encounter with an old "mossback." Wading barefoot in knee-deep water, I had flung my three fly cast out where the current would carry it down to the depths. Standing expectantly in the soft light of early morning I followed the trail of the line where it pierced the surface.

Suddenly it straightened and the heavy strike, sharply bowed rod and protesting reel seemed to happen all at once. I knew instantly that I was into something big and nearly lost the battle right then by tightening up too firmly. Fortunately, the trout was well-hooked. A couple of vicious head shakes made me realize that I should let him take some line if I were ever to land him. Back and forth he surged through the depths of the long pool, with me desperately following and hanging on as best I could.

Finally the fish began to weaken. As I steered him toward

shore he wallowed heavily, trying to turn back to deeper water but I gambled on the strain I thought the leader would take and slowly forced him toward the shallows. He made one last effort to get away, then suddenly the fight left him. Sliding him ashore I pounced on him like a hungry otter.

It was a proud moment when I entered our kitchen, wet and muddy, triumphantly holding the big 25 inch, five pound cutthroat for mother to admire. Actually, in all the years since that I've fished I've only taken one other of the blackspotted clan that was larger.

Addenda:

In grandfather's day, logging in the Bitterroot Range was selective. The watersheds were not devastated and the river has continued to produce good fishing throughout the ensuing years. The lower half of the river today also holds stocked rainbows, but the upper 50 miles or so (now designated as catch-and-release water) is still a stronghold for the original westslope cutthroat strain.

In the last few years, fishing pressure has been the only problem but present-day logging companies in the area are after the U.S.F.S. to allow clearcutting in the feeder drainages. If they are successful, the Shadowy Old St. Joe will quickly join the long and growing list of once-great angling rivers in our Northwest.

Chapter 2

Tag Alder Heaven

While I was still a lad the St. Maries mill was sold and we moved to Spokane, Washington. Among the new friends I made there was Tom Lacy. The Lacys lived three or four blocks from us and Tom's parents, Bert and Mary, treated me like one of the family. Tom and I were merely a week apart in age and when not in school spent most of our free time roaming the nearby woodlands together. He was short and well-built, a sprinter, while I was a bit taller and leaner, designed more for endurance than speed.

One of the bonds that cemented our friendship was a mutual fascination for trout fishing. We were not yet old enough to have driving licenses but there was one stream within hiking distance. On weekends we'd often coerce one of our parents to provide transportation to and from more distant trout habitats.

During the winter when we were 8th graders, Tom and I embarked on an ambitious scheme to sell Christmas trees. We had located an isolated valley full of lovely balsam fir and my mother had agreed to furnish transportation in return for fuel reimbursement (gas was then 18 cents per gallon). We canvassed all neighborhoods within reach of our southside homes, taking advance orders for trees on a "pay-only-if-satisfied" agreement.

By the time we had completed this project and had repaid mother for the gas we had the handsome sum of $10 apiece, clear profit. It doesn't sound like much now but in the days of the nickel weekly allowance it was a small fortune.

Shortly after Christmas we went downtown to one of the local sporting goods outlets and blew our hard-earned cash on twin fly fishing outfits consisting of eight foot Montague "Black Beauty" split bamboo rods with extra tip sections and single-action nickel-plated reels. That rod became my pride and joy and served me well for many years.

Tom's family had a summer cabin on Priest Lake in northern Idaho, about 90 miles northeast of Spokane. The cabin was on Luby Bay near the southwestern end of the lake. The only other settlement at that time was the tiny outpost of Coolin, across the lake near its southeastern end. Priest Lake is 16 miles long, averages four to five miles in width and is dotted with several large islands.

A dozen streams feed the lake, most flowing down the flanks of the Selkirk Mountains to the east. The upper end is fed by the Little Priest River that crosses the border between British Columbia and Idaho some 20 miles to the north. These crystalline waters had heavy populations of westslope cutthroat and Dolly Varden char, plus less numerous numbers of rainbow and brook trout.

When the interminable school year finally ended, Bert and Mary would drive Tom and me, along with two other boyhood friends, Don Walker and Walt Hayfield, to the cabin. We would spend the following two weeks fishing and exploring. The Lacys had a 16-foot outboard motorboat that we used to get to the inlets of the various streams. From a tent camp at the mouth we'd hike and fish up these watercourses.

The east side streams were mainly of the fast, Rocky Mountain type. On the west side, emptying into the Priest River just below its outflow from the lake, was a stream entirely different in character, unforgettable as the greatest producer of sizable Eastern brook trout we ever knew.

Lamb Creek was a two hour hike from Luby Bay. Its branches came out of heavily forested hills through brush-choked valleys, fed along their courses with many cold springs. At intervals, beavers backed up stretches with their well-engineered dams. Between them it was a head-deep, twisting, slow-moving meadow stream. There were very few access spots to it, most of its length being encased in heavy tangles of alder and willow. Looking at the expanse of the main Lamb Creek basin from a bordering ridge line is a lot like parachute jumping: you don't really know what you're getting into and once committed there is little chance for retreat. From any hillside take-off point we had to fight our way through a quarter mile of this jungle growth not knowing where the watercourse was until nearly falling into it.

Wriggling through this morass until we found semi-open spots then getting a lure into the water without getting hung up, disturbing the fish or falling in was the plan of attack. There was still the problem of successfully derricking out a sizable trout once hooked. Every fish safely brought to hand was a small triumph. To most adults it would be considered a tag alder hell. We boys just took it in stride.

This was no territory for fly fishing. Even the beaver ponds were solidly brushed in. Our weapons here were metal telescoping rods, bait casting reels loaded with black braided squidding line and short gut leaders, terminating with Indiana or Pearl Red Dot spinners and garden hackle. We did not have waders and much of our fishing there was on hands and knees, carefully lowering the bait through any possible opening into the deep, black currents.

Lamb Creek was heavily populated with brookies. They usually took the bait with abandon but landing them in that lattice-work of limbs was far from easy. The average size of these trout was 10 inches but there were many in the 15 to 16 inch range. Occasionally we'd luck into one of 18 inches, although most fish of that size were almost impossible to land. They could not be "horsed" out and either tore off by wrapping the leader around a sunken limb or root, or flopped off when the attempt was made to hoist them out to where they could be grabbed.

When we emerged several hours later, sweaty, fly-bitten and disheveled we always had the satisfying pressure of a heavy creel's shoulder strap as compensation. I cannot recall a single time when we came out empty-handed; we always took fish and always had managed to land several 13 to 16 inch slabs, as we called them. Those Lamb Creek inhabitants were among the deepest bodied brook trout I've ever seen, a 16 incher weighing about two pounds. Their dark olive backs, sides sprinkled with vivid yellow vermiculations and scarlet dotted blue aureoles above the white-edged fins were a joy to behold. As table fare their dark orange flesh was delicious. The evening meals that Mary Lacy prepared from them were beyond comparison.

At that time (early 1930s) the daily limit for trout was 25, having been reduced not long before from 30. In the beginning, because the limit was 25, we had to go for it. That didn't last long, however. We realized this was really in excess of our needs and thereafter stopped when we had, first 15 and later a dozen, fish. In retrospect, if the limit had been set at 10 I'm sure we would have been perfectly satisfied with that.

Over a long period of time the catch limits were reduced but state fish and game departments generally were much too late with such regulation changes. This inevitably led to overkill of probably hundreds of thousands of the resource.

Addenda:

Today, really wild trout are rapidly vanishing from the American scene and many of our best remaining waters are reduced to stock-and-take or catch-and-release regulations. Overkill is of course just one factor in the loss. In Priest Lake, the introduction of Mackinaw or lake trout resulted in a great reduction in cutthroat populations. In checking annual fish regulations, I've noted for a long time now that the majority of Priest's feeder streams are completely closed to all fishing.

Continuing destruction or defilement of trout habitat by clear-cutting loggers, dam builders and developers is steadily making more miles of streams and rivers uninhabitable for trout every year. I know of a great many waters which within the span of my years have been reduced from highly productive fisheries to warm, polluted, troutless ditches. The price of progress can indeed be high.

Chapter 3

POOLS OF MEMORY

Secret Places

All young boys have secret hideaways. Penrod had his old barn. Tom Sawyer and Huck Finn had a cave. Balser had a huge hollow sycamore. For a modern urban lad it could be a small room in an abandoned building. A rural teenager might have a little-known farm pond full of bird song, spring peepers and hungry bass.

For Tom, Don, Walt and me it was a forested glen called Paradise Valley, containing a step-across brooklet named, of course, Paradise Creek.

The valley was no more than a three hour hike from our South Manito homes in Spokane, out across the High Drive and down the steep slopes to Hangman Creek bridge, across the bordering truck gardens, up the 195 Parkway then off on an obscure dirt road that led into the lower end of the glen. Although less than a mile from a well-traveled highway the three mile length of the valley was secluded, quiet and virtually unknown. We had come across it quite by accident during one of our "Lewis and Clark" exploratory hikes.

In all the time we spent there in those early years the only other human we met was a very old and very unkempt hermit who lived in a tiny shack near the head of the valley. There were, however, a host of smaller inhabitants: a few whitetail deer, cottontails, porcupines, red squirrels, Columbian ground squirrels, ruffed grouse and many lesser-known birds such as the hawk owl, pygmy owl and Steller's jay.

The miniature stream had its beginnings in a number of hillside springs at the head of the valley. After tumbling over a rock ledge in a four foot fall it twisted, turned and bubbled down through the forested glen like a long vein of silver ore; its spongy banks filtered with fern and alder and filled with shadow drifts, back-eddy whispers and mysterious undercut bank bends. About halfway down its course, the brook was strengthened by a smaller spring-fed rill coming from a side hill cleft. After meandering out the lower end of the valley it ran under the highway and emptied into Hangman Creek through a maze of brush that completely camouflaged its presence.

Every run, every tiny pool, every underwater obstruction became an intimate segment of our association with Paradise Creek. This was especially true for Don Walker and me, for during a couple of long summers when Tom and Walt were elsewhere we spent countless days wandering through the valley glades. Sometimes we hunted grouse or ground squirrels, or explored small caves along the western ramparts of the valley rim but our main effort was directed in outwitting a few of the lovely strain of wild rainbow trout inhabiting the brook. As befitted their surroundings they were for the most part tiny fish, seven or eight inches being an average size. There was always the chance, however, of a take from a handsome, hook-jawed 10 or 12 incher.

Paradise Creek.

Certainly in those days we had no qualms about keeping fish to eat but in Paradise Creek we seldom kept more than four fish on any given outing. Only once in the years we fished there was a trout over a foot long taken. I landed a veritable monster of 20 inches from a deeply undercut bend. It was the only fish we ever took from that water that had no distinctive parr marks along its sides. I suspect it had made its way up into the brook from Hangman Creek, although how it had survived in that larger but even then highly polluted stream was a mystery.

Due to the congested conditions of stealthy crawling approaches to brush-shrouded lies, then attempting to thread the line through tiny openings, normal fishing tackle was impractical. Even our tried and true telescoping rods were too big for the job. Therefore, our Paradise Creek angling outfit was an adaptation suited to the close quarter obstacles. The pole was a four foot length of slim alder, trimmed of its twigs, to which was affixed an equal length of leader material ending with a small (size 14) snelled hook. Bait was a single salmon egg completely hiding the hook on which it was threaded. Often we'd chum a pool, dropping in a free egg or two before following up with the baited hook.

Hooking fish was not too difficult. Landing them was. On the average we probably lost two or three fish for every one we caught, the lost ones invariably being the larger specimens. Once hooked and lost, these trout became more selective in their feeding. A few lost on salmon eggs were later fooled with small grasshoppers or a segment of worm but any fish that was hooked and got away more than once became nearly impossible to deceive again for the remainder of that season.

It was certainly a far cry from fly fishing a good sized river or bait fishing a medium-sized stream, but the intimacy of the surroundings and close quarter encounters with game and fish undisturbed by other than ourselves had an allure and fascination that never waned. As angling author A. J. McClane once stated: "There is a pastoral charm to fishing small brooks and no matter how many rivers you wade, there will always be the need for coming back to a brook."

Have you ever heard of "guddling" for trout? Not many of my angling friends have, except for those of Scottish descent. It's an old Highland poacher's trick for capturing trout by hand without benefit of hooks, nets or other tackle, requiring both stealth and patience. I do not recall where I first heard or read of this ancient art but as it was specially adapted to smaller burns or brooks, I decided to try it in Paradise Creek.

I knew of a few small pools having undercut banks where the trout hid when disturbed. Approaching one of these spots on hands and knees I rose up from the grassy margin enough to alert a little rainbow in the center of the pool, which immediately darted out of sight under the bank. Visually marking the spot and easing out at full length, I gently thrust one hand and arm into the cool water and very slowly worked my open hand back under the bank. In a few moments I felt contact with the smooth side of the gently finning fish and began as delicately as possible to stroke the underside of the little trout with my finger tips. At the first touches the finning action was somewhat agitated, then it became more calm. At this stage I very, very slowly closed my hand around the now quiescent fish, being careful not to squeeze too hard, brought it out of the water and laid the seven inch troutling on the grass.

The moment my hand contact was removed, the fish began thrashing around as a normally landed trout would and to prevent any damage I gently scooped him back in the water. It had all happened so quietly and easily that for a minute I found it difficult to absorb the fact that I had actually caught a wild trout by hand.

In trying the trick several times again, I was sufficiently successful with fish up to 12 inches long that I could have obtained enough to eat in a survival situation.

I have not done this again as an adult preferring to tempt the fish with a home-tied fly on a gossamer leader. Somehow and I can't really explain this, I have the feeling that guddling should only be tried by youngsters.

I had another secret place a bit later on, this one mine alone. At 14, thanks to patient tutoring by mother, I had learned to drive, had obtained a license and could occasionally use one of the family cars, a rumble-seated Packard coupe. With it I was able to venture further afield. While exploring back roads one weekend near the Idaho state line, I came upon another small brook about the size of Paradise Creek. Appropriately enough, I first crossed it in heavy woodlands on a road whose sign proclaimed it to be Lost Trail Road. So of course the miniature waterway immediately became Lost Creek to me.

A half mile after crossing the creek the road forked to right and left. Taking the left fork, I drove up a hill and soon came to a farm with large pastures in the valley below. I could see from this viewpoint that the stream flowed through these Guernsey-speckled meadows. Driving into the farmyard, I asked permission of the owner to fish.

"Well," he said, "I don't rightly know if there's any fish in there but you're welcome to try. Just watch out for that big bull in the lower pasture. He can be ornery."

Thanking him I grabbed my telescoping rod, split willow creel and Prince Albert can of worms and headed down across the meadow. The watercourse here was narrow but the water was deep, dark and mysterious. I found out almost immediately that it was loaded with lovely brook trout. Every pool yielded a fish or two to my searching spinner and worm and in less than an hour I had a dozen of the green-backed, orange-bellied beauties, from 10 to 14 inches, cleaned and resting in a bed of fresh watercress. Stopping again at the farmhouse, I gave a half dozen to the farmer's wife. She in turn plied me with apple pie and coffee and invited me back to fish anytime.

That was an invitation I certainly took advantage of. On later trips I fished different stretches of the creek, finding the bright brookies abundant everywhere. I tried the guddling trick and succeeded in landing several fish in this manner.

One interesting expanse of stream toward the end of the lower pasture ran underground for a hundred yards with here and there a small opening to the water, around a stump or tree roots. It was exciting beyond description to sneak quietly up to these openings, lower the baited hook gently down to the sandy bottom and watch a trout dart in from the covered recesses to seize it avidly. It then became quite a struggle to get the fish out through the opening without losing him. It was much like ice fishing, except that I could see what was going on under the surface.

One day, as a result of being so wrapped up in the fishing action that I failed to notice what was going on around me, I nearly came to grief. The large resident-bull resented my intrusion into his domain and I barely made it to a small copse of aspens before he got to me. From a distance the farmer spotted my predicament and drove down across the meadow on his tractor. He picked up a spare cedar fence post and rapped the bull over the head. This made little impression on the animal except for a bit of grunting and pawing turf. After a couple more solid raps, however, the bull decided he'd met his match and slowly moved off across the meadow. "Just got to show 'em who's boss," the farmer remarked as he climbed back on his tractor.

Addenda:

In such small waters, far from the involvements of technological research and business-like pursuit of large, sophisticated prey one comes closest to the simple delight and fascination of one's true beginnings in the sport. Returning to a former secret hideaway may be disillusioning and even shocking.

In another year or so we moved from Washington to a distant state and it was only after years of absence that I returned to the area and made a side trip to Paradise Valley. The road into the valley had been widened and graded. I immediately ran into colored stakes driven in the ground and plastic streamers tied to tree branches. The developers had moved in. Much of the larger timber, mostly yellow pine, had been cut. There was no trace of the lovely but delicate Yellow Bells and Grass Widows that had once bloomed there in profusion. The scene was totally unlike the one I remembered.

A bit further up the valley I ran into a string of houses. The owners had of course cleaned out all of the understory and had planted lawns down to the denuded stream banks. Two of the home owners had dammed the stream with planks and cement blocks to form pools for their yards. One home had horses penned in a pole corral that spanned the creek.

Still further up the valley, more clearing had been done and the unshaded water had warmed. In the few spots I tried fishing I found no sign of life, although I suppose there are perhaps a few surviving fish in some out-of-the-way undercut tangles. I saw no deer, grouse, owls, hawks, jays, ground squirrels or other wildlife. Only a couple of red squirrels were in evidence which was not too surprising given the severely altered habitat. I realized then, as I have confirmed several times since, the truth of the declaration by Thomas Wolfe that you can never go back to find things the same.

Such progress can't be stopped but it's too bad it can't. Too bad the human species has to play God and in its accelerating greed denude the habitats so necessary to other forms of life.

Chapter 4

Hod Connor's Ponds

y first really exotic angling adventure occurred in 1935 when I was a freshman in high school. During the summer vacation, our parents took my younger brother Bob and me on a trip to Michigan. While there we stayed a week or so with our cousins, Redge Moll and his family, in the Upper Peninsula village of Bruce Crossing.

Also staying with Redge that summer was his lifelong companion, Tommy Cole. Both men were dedicated outdoorsmen, Redge raised Labrador retrievers, tied trout flies professionally and, with Tommy, had worked for the Michigan Department of Conservation in predator trapping and other wildlife management programs. Both men were fly fishers. Tommy Cole was a bachelor whose home was in the iron mining town of Ishpeming. It was there that he converted another friend, John Voelker, from bait fishing to fly angling and later became one of the central figures in John's popular fishing novels (published under the name of Robert Traver).

Redge and Tommy educated me. One of the first things they did was teach me to tie flies which I took to like a trout takes to caddis. From there, they instructed me in all the art and nuances of fly fishing including the proper use of small bucktails and streamers. I soon found these to be highly effective on the brook trout of the Middle Branch of the Ontonagon, the Jumbo River, the Baltimore, the Whitefish and other nearby waters.

Finally one overcast, muggy and buggy evening in July Redge told me to get my tackle ready, that we were going to hike in to a special place. I had no idea just how special a spot it would turn out to be.

Daylight was beginning to fade as we drove from Bruce Crossing to Kenton, 20 miles to the east. Kenton is a very small village on the banks of the East Branch of the Ontonagon River, having remained quiescent since the passing of the white pine logging era. It was here my paternal grandfather had started his career as a lumberman.

From Kenton Redge took a side road north for several miles, at one point passing over a likely looking stretch of stream that meandered through a natural hay meadow. Redge said it was called Beaver Creek, for reasons I would later see, and emptied into the East Branch a short distance away. He also mentioned that where we were going to fish had, years ago, been a favorite spot of my grandfather's. That bit of news in itself made the hair on the back of my neck rise—I was about to fish where my grandfather had fished more than a quarter of a century before.

Redge finally pulled the car over to the edge of the bush road and we started off on foot through the woods, following what looked like an old game trail. After a 15 or 20 minute hike we could hear the sound of running water and emerged upon a scene that took my breath away. It was unlike anything I'd ever seen before, yet somehow seemed strangely familiar. As Yogi Berra said: "It was like deja vu all over again."

We were standing near the end of a huge beaver dam with ponds both above and below it. The dam itself was 12 to 15 feet high and almost completely sodded over with tag alder, ferns and grasses sprouting from its lattice-work of logs. It was obviously very old. The beaver had been there when grandfather and the young lad who would become my father initially saw the stream and traveled first by horse and buggy, then by shank's mare, to fish the ponds.

Climbing up on the dam I could see water backed up for at least a quarter of a mile, with many dead but still standing trees along its sides. The water was black as pitch and very deep—certainly impossible to wade. I stood transfixed, staring out over the magnificent scene. In my direct line of sight, beside a huge old white pine stump, a brook trout suddenly breached the surface. It was the biggest brookie I had ever seen and was larger than any I thought ever grew.

I suddenly wanted that fish more than anything I had ever previously desired. Yet I was completely foiled, for it was beyond my casting ability and there was no way I could get closer.

As I stood there in a spellbound stupor other fish, big fish, began rolling everywhere. I heard Redge shout and turning around saw him hip deep in the lower pond and fast to a sizable trout. He hollered something about getting my ass down there while the fish were active. I could barely make out what he said above the noise of water flowing through the depths of the dam.

Scrambling down, I waded out near him and cast a Grizzly King wet fly out among the rolling trout. Almost immediately it was taken. In my eagerness I struck too hard and lost both fish and fly.

In the time it took me to tie on another fly Redge had landed two or three lovely, deep-bodied brookies. He was fishing with two flies, a tail and a dropper, and hooked a fish of about 16 inches on the dropper. As he was attempting to subdue it, another fish hit the tail fly and that one was a real squaretail. I got a good look at it when the action surged my way. Redge later said it was a four pounder that he had encountered before and I had no reason whatever to doubt him. At any rate, the double tie-up ended in disaster as the tail fish surged one way and the dropper fish another. Something had to give and, of course, it was the larger trout that tore off. The air in Redge's vicinity turned deep purple for a moment or two.

By the time darkness settled in we had a catch of brook trout that dreams are made of. I had six and Redge had 10. None was less than a pound and a half; the largest being 20 inches and three pounds: gorgeous, dark, heavy, lantern-jawed fish whose bejewelled flanks and white-edged fins were breathtaking.

Packing our fish in creels lined with wet pond-side ferns we took the trail back out through the gathering gloom, accompanied by the melancholy seven note rise and fall of a whitethroat's evening song.

I subsequently fished the ponds a few more times, on each occasion catching a few large, lovely trout but never again did I encounter a rise of fish like the one of that first magical evening.

Addenda:
Before the decade of the 1930s was over, a tragic end came to these ponds. Someone in the State Fish & Game Department decided that all beaver dams everywhere were ruinous to both fishing and real estate and in 1934 ordered the Civilian Conservation Corps to blow out all of the dams they could find. Redge later told me the C.C.C. camp that had dynamited the Hod Connor dams had afterwards gathered many washtubs of big trout for their mess hall.

Beaver Creek is still there and still contains brook trout, although habitat destruction and the introduction of brown trout have reduced the population and the fish size from pounds to inches.

Sic transit gloria.

Chapter 5 POOLS OF MEMORY
The Outlet Run

The 1935 summer vacation that our family spent in Michigan was the real beginning of my fly fishing career. It came to a temporary halt in August, as we had to get back to our Spokane home in time for my brother and me to start the fall school term. We did have a few days to spare, however, and persuaded dad to make a slight detour through Yellowstone Park on the way.

While in the park we spent a couple of nights in a rental cabin near the old Fishing Bridge which spanned the Yellowstone River a short distance below its outflow from the lake. At that time the bridge was still the original log construction and fishing was allowed from both above and below it. One could stand at the bridge railing and watch dozens of fine black-spotted cutthroat finning gently in the placid currents below. Lines of tourists fished from the bridge, usually using salmon eggs as bait, and at times there were some real entanglements. Hooking one another in the ear was not uncommon.

The morning after we checked into our cabin I arose before daylight, quietly dressed and gathered my gear and headed for the river. Dawn was just breaking when I arrived at the bridge. A heavy mist lay over the river. At that hour I had it all to myself. Crossing to the north side of the river, I waded in about halfway between the lake outlet and the bridge. The water was cold on my waderless legs and formed a long run rather than being defined into riffles and pools. Its currents were strong but the surface was smooth. The contour of the river bed was such that I was able to wade about 30 yards out without getting more than hip deep and from there could cast nearly to the center of the run.

Fog was still hanging low and hid the far side of the river from view when a succession of memorable moments began. The first occurred as I was tying a fly to my leader. Hearing a sudden whish, whish, whish, I looked up in time to see a small wedge of Canadian geese emerge from the downstream mists just before they flew directly over me not more than 50 feet above the river. Their alarm calls drifted back as they disappeared over the curtained expanse of Yellowstone Lake. I was conscious at the time of imprinting the scene on my memory so that I would never forget,

26

and I never have. The secretive, enveloping mist and the close passage of wild geese through it aroused and intensified a vague, undefinable sense of being an integral part of my surroundings.

A field note reminds me that the fly I used that day was one I had tied on Redge Moll's vise. A nondescript pattern on a size 8 hook it sported a short red tail, yellow chenille body ribbed with peacock herl, short wing of gray squirrel tail and brown hackle. I assume the fish mistook it for a grasshopper. Take it they did! I had made less than a half dozen casts before a hard strike doubled the rod over while the line hissed audibly through the water, leaving a sharp V wake as it went.

While I instinctively yielded line to the trout's surges, and gained a few feet back when possible, another sound registered. Something heavy was moving through the water toward me. A dark object emerged from the mist directly in front of me. I discovered it to be the head and shoulders of a large bear.

I was frozen with indecision: I wanted to move out of his way but had my hands full with the hooked trout. When some 15 or 20 yards from me the bear finally realized from the dancing rod and moving arms that what he saw was not just a tree stub. With a loud "Woof!" he swung slightly downstream and passed closely by me. His wet hair seemed very dark and I assumed it was a black bear until I saw his shoulder hump and dished face in profile. It was the closest encounter I ever had with a mature grizzly and I'm sure he was as startled by the experience as I was. Reaching the shore behind me, he shook himself like a big dog and disappeared over the bank.

I landed the fish, a beautiful two pound cutthroat, and within the hour had my limit of five which furnished breakfast for our family and for the cook at the nearby lodge who graciously prepared them for us.

The best thing about the entire episode was the fact that I had caught my first fish on a fly I had tied. Aldo Leopold once stated: "A home-tied fly enhances the sport—he who kills a trout with his own fly has scored two coups, not one."

Addenda:
During those early days, tons of Yellowstone cutthroat ended up in the park's garbage cans after being caught and held up or laid out for boastful snapshots. This slaughter got so bad that park officials finally decreed no more fishing from or near the bridge and instigated a catch-and-release program on much of the Yellowstone River and other heavily fished streams within the park.

Chapter 6

Tommy's Hole

I n 1936, when I was a sophomore in high school, our family split up. Mother, my brother Bob and I moved back to the old MacKenzie home in Negaunee, Michigan which had been left to mother by her parents.

It was rather a sad time but it proved to be a fortuitous move as far as my angling career was concerned. Tommy Cole and John Voelker lived in Ishpeming, just three miles away, and the Moll home in Bruce Crossing was a two hour drive. Scores of fine fishing opportunities surrounded us; locally renowned rivers such as the Big Dead, Escanaba, Mulligan, Yellow Dog, Big West, Ontonagon, Chocolay, plus many smaller streams, ponds and beaver impoundments on their feeder brooks. These were all native brook trout habitat. It would be a few years before the Fish & Game Department began introducing browns and rainbows on a large scale. As has been proven many times brook trout, like the western cutthroat, are a noncompetitive species. When other fish are stocked in their waters brookies often become scarce or disappear.

All the anglers I knew were happy to have the beautiful brookies. True, they didn't grow to the size of other trout, but size is really their least important quality. When prepared for the table a 10 inch brook trout is far more delectable than a brown or rainbow of any size.

Up above the Mulligan River plains the Big Dead River flows into and out of a large body of water called Silver Lake. At the lake's outlet is a hydroelectric dam that was put in many years ago by the Cleveland Cliffs Iron Mining Company. Dan Spencer, the protagonist of many of John Voelker's tales, was caretaker of the dam. His main job was to be on hand to release water from the lake during summertime needs brought about by rainless periods and resulting in low river levels. The caretaker's cabin adjacent to the dam was the only habitation on the lake. The remainder of the shoreline was sheathed in groves of balsam, spruce and pine. To get to the upper end of the lake where the headwaters of the Big Dead entered, one could either hike up an old overgrown bush road or use a canoe.

Silver Lake was noted for its smallmouth bass but most fishermen did not realize it also contained a population of huge squaretailed brook trout. The latter were seldom encountered, evidently staying most of the time in or near deep water spring holes.

Where the heavy current of the Big Dead entered, it had worn a deep channel for some distance out into the lake. This set the stage for the big secret of Silver Lake which at that time was known to very few.

When he was given orders from the C.C.I. to release lake water, Dan Spencer would phone Tommy Cole and a small expedition to the lake would immediately take place. In such occasional late summer periods the lowering surface level caused the usually submerged inlet channel to become exposed. When this happened, and other conditions of water temperature, barometric pressure and insects hatching were right, flotillas of huge brook trout would emerge from the lake depths and move up into the channel at dusk, feeding voraciously as they advanced. At such times one could reach the risers by wading out into the lake on either side of the channel.

Tommy was a superb fly fisherman. As he invariably seemed to be "top rod" at this inlet stretch it became known to his few angling confederates as Tommy's Hole. I wish I could produce a copy of one of the photo prints Tom Cole had showing a catch of these squaretails laid out in a washtub, tails touching one side and heads the other. Those are big brookies in anyone's lexicon.

These channel invasions were unique in that the trout

With Tommy Cole—frying up a few freshly caught brookies.

involved were all surface feeding. It was one of the few instances I've known when dry flies were more effective than wets for large brook trout. It was also one of the most thrilling and nerve-wracking times a squaretail lover could possibly experience, huge fish breaking the surface all around him in tremendous boiling rises. The main difficulty was that the trout would not take a fly tied to a heavy leader and if the leader were light enough to fool them it was seldom strong enough to hold them. Leaders then were not of the quality they are today and a maze of underwater debris washed in by the river added further complications. It was one of the worst fly and tippet graveyards I ever experienced.

Actually, I was a Tommy's Hole expedition member on just one occasion when conditions were right but I will never forget the sheer excitement, bordering on hysteria, engendered by hooking, then losing, one huge trout after another. Anyone who believes brook trout do not fight as well as other trout just hasn't tangled with any sizable brookies. When the all-too-brief rise ended that evening I had landed just one fish. A three pounder, it was the largest brook trout I had ever taken to that point but the other members of our expedition, Tommy, Pinky Strand and Johnny Voelker had all landed fish a pound or two larger than mine.

It was a mind-bending adventure for a 16-year-old. During the ensuing celebration I was offered and accepted my first spirituous libation.

Time staggered on.

Chapter 7
The Big West and Chandler Brook

While I was still in high school there were brook trout everywhere in Michigan's Upper Peninsula. Much of the region consists of Precambrian rock, swamps, bogs, marshes and land generally unfit to raise anything except marsh hay, potato patches and other garden vegetables, dairy cattle and crops of wildlife. There were, and still are, very few towns of any size and long stretches of second growth forest between them, liberally sprinkled with both running and standing waterways.

Iron ore had first been discovered in Negaunee in 1844 and the resulting mines were still in their heyday. Many of the miners were of Finnish stock, having chosen to live in the U.P. because of the similarity in terrain and climate to their homeland.

Among the friends my brother Bob and I made in school were the Aho brothers, Paul and Bill, and another Finnish lad named Paul Kauppinen. A mutual love of hunting and fishing was the cement that bound our friendship.

The year after our family move to Negaunee (1937) the State Fish & Game Department opened the first state-wide bow hunting season for whitetail deer and we were among the earliest scattered hunters in our area to take up this "new" sport.

While autumn bow season lasted less than a month our trout fishing could be carried on all spring and summer. There were other considerable differences. The ratio of success was far greater against trout. While putting a broadhead into a game animal is normally pretty final the strike and hooking of a game fish is only the beginning, with the outcome not nearly as certain. We enjoyed both sports but trout fishing remained the favorite pastime. I conveyed my relatively new knowledge of fly tying to the Ahos and they quickly became proficient tiers.

While our fishing expeditions ranged far and wide, thanks to a dependable Model A sedan Paul Aho had acquired, one area in particular became our favorite. In Section 4 of Wells Township in the southeastern part of Marquette County, the Big Brook and the North Branch came together to form the Big West River. Further fed by the West Branch and Chandler Brook the Big West flowed some 10 miles before emptying into the middle branch of the Escanaba River.

The Big West, one of the loveliest of midwestern rivers.

It was about a two hour drive from Negaunee, through the villages of Palmer and Suomi, past Gwinn and the Shag Lakes to where County Road 557 crossed the Big West. This is a sizable river, averaging 50 yards in width, and is largely a succession of wadeable, sandy-bottomed pools and swift, gravelly riffles interspersed with a few deeper and calmer stretches. It looks more like a Montana or Wyoming river than any other eastern stream I know of. Its entire course was through heavy hardwood and evergreen woodlands.

At that time there was one small farm near the bridge but no camps on the river and we seldom encountered other fishermen there. I never quite understood this, as the river not only supported a healthy population of brook trout but many were of the size generally found only in ponds or beaver flowages. Sixteen to 18 inch fish were always a possibility.

The best fly patterns were small streamers tied on size 8 or 10 hooks, our favorites being the Black Ghost, Yellow Tiger, Royal Coachman, Cosseboom and Undertaker.

During this period I had read about John Alden Knight's

Solunar Theory in angling periodicals, its premise being that the varying phases of the moon affect not only earthly tides but also influence all life forms on our planet. One of its results was the demarcation of major and minor feeding periods of game fish. Although I was dubious I decided to test it out one summer.

The *Marquette Mining Journal* published solunar table information for a week in advance in each Saturday's edition. I began clipping out this information and carrying it in my fishing vest. I did not schedule my outings according to the tables, being a firm believer in the "go fishing every chance you get" school. All summer I did check the table's notations every time the trout were responding well to my presentation. At the end of the season my field notes showed that, without exception, my most successful hours corresponded with major feeding periods as noted in the tables.

Other influences such as high or low pressure fronts with sudden drops or rises in the barometer can somewhat negate the effects of the moon's pull, but I found the tables to be remarkably accurate.

Since that summer, despite remaining a believer, I've never again fished according to the solunar theory. The reason is simple: I still believe more firmly in taking my chances regardless of weather or other conditions. "Aye, fishing's the end in itself," grandfather MacKenzie might have said.

Fishing in the Big West was best just after the spring runoff although we fished it at various times throughout the season. We came to realize that during the hot dog days of late summer most fish migrated up the cooler feeder streams and it was during our explorations involving these that we really struck it rich.

We discovered an old bush road that led into a hidden stretch of Chandler Brook. The brook was large but overgrown with alders and did not appear impressive. It looked more like chub and sucker habitat, running slow and deep over a largely black muck bottom. Appearances, however, can be as deceiving in streams as in people. The very first cast I made into the Chandler was a sloppy one, the line and Michigan Hopper fly splatting down heavily at the edge of a grassy overhang. No sooner had it hit the surface than the fly was sucked under in a boiling rise. After a short but spirited tussle, I netted a darkly-shaded 15 inch brookie, its silky sides glowing with wildflower hues. It was a fine beginning and on several more occasions that day when I placed my fly in tight to the opposite bank, a bulging wake would emerge from the undercut and inexorably close on the yellow-bodied hopper pattern. My companions fared as well.

On our earliest trips to the Chandler we fished it downstream to where it joined the Big West. Because of the soft muck bottom and heavily brushed-in banks it was hard work but the beautiful trout we occasionally took were well worth the effort. There was one day, however, when the trek nearly ended in disaster.

Paul Aho and I had driven out to our usual parking spot, from where a deer trail led some hundred yards to the banks of the brook. We started downstream with our habitual leapfrogging technique. One of us would fish through a stretch of a hundred yards or so while the other detoured around through the brush to get in the stream some distance below. When the upper fisherman caught up with his companion, it would be his turn to get out and reenter downstream.

On this particular day I was engrossed in trying to work my fly in under overhanging alders when Paul, who had struck off through the thickets, began to holler. I instantly recognized his cries as those of fright and pain. The first thought that crossed my mind was, "A bear! He'd come across a sow with cubs!"

"Hang on," I shouted as I sloshed up the stream bank, "I'm coming!"

"Don't come in here!" came back loud and clear, followed by more hollering and crashing of brush.

Coaxing one in on the Chandler Brook.

Making my way down around the bend, I came upon Paul in the brook. His shirt and fishing vest were off and he was gouging handfuls of mud from the bottom and slapping them on various parts of his body. I couldn't understand the situation until I got close enough to see his puffed-up face. He had stumbled into a ground nest of bald-faced hornets and had stings all over his upper body, evidenced by quarter-sized white blotches with red centers.

In his retreat Paul had lost his glasses, his creel and net and his fly rod, but he wasn't about to go back in there after them. After waiting about 30 minutes to give his adversaries a chance to calm down, I very carefully sneaked back to the scene of the attack and retrieved Paul's equipment, seeing a few of the large black and white hornets but avoiding contact. The tip section of Paul's rod was broken, as were his glasses, but our fishing was over for the day anyway.

On our next trip to Chandler Brook Paul and I ventured upstream from the starting point. We hadn't gone more than a quarter of a mile before coming to a large beaver pond. Paul had reached the pond first and by the time I got there in response to his call, he had already hooked a large trout that was trying to turn his fly rod into a hairpin. It didn't take me long to join the action. Before my companion had landed his fish I was solidly into another slab-sided brookie. In an hour we had each taken five fish, most of which completely spanned the bottom of our 16 inch creels.

There, and for beaver ponds generally, one of the most reliable wet fly patterns was the Grizzly King, tied with a short gray squirrel tail wing. We later discovered a couple of smaller ponds upstream from the first one and had several wonderful catches from them, always stopping when we each had five trout.

Then we made a bad mistake. We invited another classmate, one who occasionally bow hunted with us, on an excursion to the Chandler after getting his promise that he would not tell anyone else.

The following weekend Paul went out alone to the ponds and ran directly into our "friend," along with his entire family, busy filling gunny sacks with the lovely brookies they were taking with gobs of nightcrawlers.

That was the end of a friendship and, unfortunately, the ponds never did come back. That moronic tribe continued to fish the ponds until all the trout were gone.

Addenda:

Chandler Brook still flows. The beaver ponds are still there, reduced in size and full of chubs, with only an occasional small troutling. As with many similar waters of former greatness it shows signs of relentless pressure as mutely attested to by the empty bait cartons, tangles of monofilament, beer cans and other debris along its banks.

Paul and I still get together occasionally and make a pilgrimage from his Iron Mountain home to the Big West and Chandler Brook. Now it is pure nostalgia that draws us back, rather than the promise of good fishing.

Chapter 8

Kenai Encounter

U pon graduating from Negaunee High School I embarked on one of the busiest periods of my life, attending college winters and working summers to earn tuition.

I began this educational struggle at the University of Idaho. Three factors influenced my move back West. First, it was the state of my birth. Second, I wanted to major in Zoology, which was offered there, and third, my childhood chum, Tom Lacy, was also enrolling at that time in their School of Forestry.

While at Idaho I spent two summers working for the U.S. Forest Service and, in both cases, was fortunate in being assigned to wilderness areas in the Couer d'Alene National Forest that had nearly virginal trout fishing opportunities.

After those first two years my educational efforts were interrupted by "greetings" from Uncle Sam. I ended up "on tour" with the Army Corps of Engineers in North Africa, Sicily and Italy for the following three years.

Fortunately, I got back in one piece with the knowledge that the G.I. Bill would allow me to finish my schooling. I immediately ran into a snag. Applications to the University of Idaho and University of Washington were both turned down—like practically all the larger state colleges, they were filled to capacity.

I had read somewhere that the University of Alaska, while a small school, had highly accredited teachers. As I had always wanted to get up there I applied and was accepted.

Shortly after my army service discharge I had purchased a 1943 Chevrolet coupe for a little over $600. The following summer was spent touring the West with my brother Bob and Paul Kauppinen. Trout fishing and exploration were the main activities. The Yellowstone and Grand Teton regions in particular were still uncrowded and we enjoyed wonderful sport in many of their off-the-beaten-path waters.

We ended up that fall in Seattle, where we split up. Bob and Paul found jobs in the logging industry while I put my car on a freighter and sailed up the Inside Passage to Valdez. The fare for the car and myself was $200. At Valdez I unloaded and drove over the mountains on the still-under-construction Richardson Highway to Fairbanks.

That winter was the greatest term of my schooling days. Total enrollment at the university was 300, the majority of whom were World War II veterans like myself. Classes were small and informal, the professors excellent and the student body was like one big happy family.

After the spring term came to a close a classmate and friend, Jim Yocum, and I got jobs with the Birch/Johnson/Lytle Company that was constructing the new Ladd Field Air Base. Jim worked on a survey crew and I drove a gravel truck. We made $5.50 an hour, could put in all the overtime we wanted at time-and-a-half and were charged $10 per week for food and lodging!

In two months we had amassed enough funds for another year of school. We decided to quit and see some of the country. Taking the train from Fairbanks to Anchorage and continuing down the Kenai Peninsula we got off at the small settlement of Moose Pass, shouldered our backpacks and took off for the Kenai River.

Headquartering near the hamlet of Cooper's Landing we hiked up and down the Kenai River and into one of its major feeders, the Russian River, searching for steelhead. We found them in plenty and had fantastic sport while meeting up with less than half a dozen other anglers. One outstanding encounter made this trip unforgettable.

The big Kenai River king salmon.

We were fishing early one morning some distance downriver from the Cooper's Landing bridge where a feeder stream ran into the Kenai near the head of a deep run. We were using weighted streamers on fairly large hooks. I had on a size 4 Skykomish Sunrise, casting it across and upstream and following its submerged drift with the rod tip held low. On the fourth or fifth drift the fly stopped in its swing, the line tightened and I struck hard. Nothing happened. I knew I was not foul-hooked on the bottom for I could feel the slow rhythmic beats of a great tail fin telegraphed through the line. Then suddenly the fish moved, steadily, seemingly unstoppable. There was no question of turning him. He just ran. When he had my fly line and some 80 yards of backing out, I began to run. When I caught up to him 200 yards downstream he was holding in a white-topped eddy behind a large midriver boulder. I put on all the pressure I dared but still could not budge him.

Then the fish started back upstream, slowly at first, but gathering momentum that ended in a tremendous leap. Seeing him for the first time, I realized that instead of a world record steelhead I was fast to a big, fresh-run king salmon. "Hell, I'll never land him," I thought. Amazingly, the inexorable pressure of the bowed rod slowly began to wear the fish down. I could feel his short surging runs against the current lacked the power of earlier efforts. Unexpectedly he turned on his side and, with Jim's help, we slid him into the shallows.

We held him long enough to remove the fly, snap a photo and weigh him on Jim's pocket scale. Nearly 30 pounds of salmon! We held him upright in the current while his gills pumped vital oxygen through his body. Finally, with a flip, he was gone.

To this day that fish remains the second largest I ever landed with a fly rod. In retrospect, it just may have been one of the first king salmon ever taken on fly fishing tackle.

Chapter 9
POOLS OF MEMORY
The Narrows

Between school sessions, in the summers of 1948 and 1949, working as a Field Biologist for the Fisheries Research Institute of Seattle, Washington I was assigned to the Bristol Bay area of Alaska to gather data on the spawning runs of sockeye salmon.

Each year's session began with time spent at a cannery, collecting biological information through random sampling of the commercial catch. This consisted mainly of sex-ratio counts, measurements taken with a special machine and recorded on rolls of paper tape, collecting any parasites found and saving scale samples for later aging.

I worked at the Wingard Cannery on the Ugashik River in 1948 and at the Alaska Packers Association Cannery on the Egegik River in 1949. Commercial salmon fishing in the Bristol Bay rivers at that time was with drift nets. No auxiliary power was allowed for the 30-foot, open decked sailboats owned by the canneries. The center section of each boat was cribbed off to carry the fish, a full load being about 4,000 salmon. The two-man crew paid out their nets across the river currents and would drift downstream until the nets were heavy with salmon. They would then anchor, haul in the nets, remove the fish and when a full load was achieved would hoist the sail and head upriver to the tally scow, or to the cannery itself, whichever was closer.

The work was cold, wet and hard and in a blow could become a nightmare. The lower river stretches were wide and smooth flowing but westerly storms frequently swept in from Bristol Bay and up the river courses with gale velocity. Fishermen caught in such a storm with nets full of salmon, or with a boat filled to the gunwales, were in real trouble. At times, nets full of fish had to be cut loose to save the boat. Many a boat, crew and load of fish were swamped and lost. During each of the two seasons I worked in the area some 15 lives were lost in this manner. It wasn't until 1952 that the drift boat crews were allowed to use auxiliary power, in the form of outboard motors.

Following the month and a half commercial fishing period, the canneries closed down. Then, a partner and I would proceed to journey up the Ugashik and the Egegik rivers to the sockeye

Bob Baade, our work boat and Arctic char from the Ugashik Narrows.

(*Oncorhynchus nerka*) spawning grounds. Our transportation was the *Nerka,* one of the 30-foot drift net boats that we had fitted with a plywood cabin housing two bunks and a small but well-stocked galley, plus a double well in the stern in which were two 10-horse power Johnson outboards.

These broad Alaskan Peninsula rivers are many miles long and are headed by large lake systems, often with stretches of rapids below the outlets. Salmon that escape the nets run up into the lakes where they spend two or three weeks in huge schools while completing the process of sexual maturing. It is during this time that the fish turn bright red (with the males assuming dark green heads and heavily kyped jaws).

By the time we had finished outfitting and had worked our way up through the first river rapids, the salmon were ascending the many feeder streams from the lake on their final procreative mission. Reaching the lake, we would travel to the mouth of a stream, anchor there, and hike up until we found a typical spawn- ing stretch. We'd mark this with strips of heavy sail canvas tied to trees and then would spend a day or two gathering the necessary data. We not only recorded measurements of all the recently expired fish on our little machine, with sex-ratio counts and scale sampling, but also documented stream gradient, flow ratio, tem- perature, bottom composition, bank strata, aquatic vegetation and other pertinent stream and watershed characteristics.

To supplement our larder ducks were plentiful, the hillsides rich with ptarmigan and game fish other than salmon were always available. In the process of procuring enough of these resources for meals we had some tremendous sport. Two spots in particular stand out in my many memories of the region.

The first was the Narrows, a half mile stretch of river separating Upper and Lower Ugashik Lakes. Where the river entered

Alaskan cohos, fish drying on rack are sockeye.

the lower lake, a large indented sand bar provided good boat anchorage. Near the lake shore was a small cabin used by the Indian family who owned it as the base for catching and drying salmon to be used as winter feed for their sled dogs, and later as shelter while running traplines. This was the only sign of human habitation in the area, the nearest neighbor being a seasonal Fish & Wildlife cabin and weir downriver from Lower Ugashik Lake. We had permission to use the stove in the Indian's cabin for baking bread; the resulting sourdough loaves being our favorite staple.

The Narrows was swift, boulder-strewn, glass-clear and ice-cold. It was also filled with incredible numbers of Arctic char, Mackinaw trout, grayling, silver or coho salmon and sockeye. Fishing this water was not only nonstop action but was real *potpourri* angling. One never knew what he'd hook into next. These were all hefty fish. The char ran eight to 10 pounds, the silvers 10 to 15, the Macks five to 20 and the grayling two to over three pounds. In one evening of hectic catch and release sport my partner and I landed about a hundred pounds of fish, saving just two, a char for fish gurry and a silver for baking.

We used both small wobbling spoons and bright patterned streamer flies except when trying for grayling, when we'd switch to small Adams, Mosquito or Black Gnat dry flies. I preferred using the fly rod, since sockeye often hit a spoon, and these were the fish we least wanted to catch. The Narrows grayling averaged larger in size than any we took elsewhere with one outstanding exception.

After a month of working the Ugashik watersheds we'd travel back down the river to Bristol Bay, motor north along the coastline to the mouth of the Egegik and run up this even larger river to Becharof Lake. Once there we traveled from stream to stream, duplicating the work done at Ugashik.

One of the streams we surveyed near the head of Lake Becharof was called Ruth Creek. Its sandy bottom and glass-clear currents were the habitat of an amazing grayling population— amazing not only in numbers but also in the average size of the fish, which ran three and a half to more than four pounds.

Size 14 gray or black patterned dry flies were the takers. Two or three of the lovely banner-dorsaled grayling we caught there were within a few ounces of five pounds.

The last stream we planned to work in 1948 was Bear Creek near the southeast end of Becharof Lake. Fall was fast closing in. The weather was becoming more unsettled every day. We made a run across the lake between the Severson Peninsula and the Gas Rocks and lined the *Nerka* up over the bar and into a small lagoon inside the stream mouth for safe anchorage.

It took two days to finish our spawning grounds work and by then the weather had turned quite nasty. We were storm-bound for an entire week, the wind and wave action making it impossible to get out on the lake. Finally, during a comparative lull, we attempted to get underway but the storm had built up the gravel bar across the creek mouth and in trying to get out over it we sheared both motor pins. At the same time we were hit with heavy breakers from a new squall and despite our best efforts the *Nerka* ended up high on the beach.

With no means to free the grounded vessel there was nothing to do but unload her and make a cache for most of the supplies and equipment, taking out just the necessities of our records, a mountain tent, sleeping bags, light rations, fishing rods and guns. The following morning we took off, backpacking along the northeastern lake shore toward the outlet some 50 miles away. It was a rough hike but in four days, during one of which we were stormbound again, we made it to a small Indian village below the outlet of the river. The chief gave us a ride down to the Egegik cannery in his boat. He later salvaged the *Nerka* and our cache.

The following year was a duplicate of the first but fortunately without any similar mishaps.

Addenda:

Since those midcentury years much of the Alaskan Peninsula's wilderness has been taken over by civilization's inroads. Although I've never returned to that area I understand there is now a large modern sportfishing lodge at the Ugashik Narrows, accessible by float plane and helicopter, offering for a price all the amenities of a comfortable, carefree outing. The fishing may still be good there but it can never again be the experience it once was. I loved that country but I'll not go back.

Chapter 10
Seven Mile Hole

POOLS OF MEMORY

After my stint at the University of Alaska I went back to Idaho and obtained my B.S. degree in the spring of 1950. A small celebration was in order.

Fellow graduate and roommate, Jim Kugler, agreed and suggested a visit to his home in Livingston, Montana from whence we'd embark on a mighty Yellowstone Park expedition. I reminded him that the official opening of the park was still two weeks away but Jim assured me that was no problem. He had worked in the park for two or three summers and knew most of the rangers, including those who manned the northwest entrance at Mammoth Hot Springs.

Jim was right. We had no trouble getting into the park and had free housekeeping cabin accommodations wherever we stayed. There we were with all those miles of trout-filled water, fish lulled into security by a long, peaceful winter and no competition from other anglers. It was like suddenly finding yourself in the middle of a high adventure movie.

We hopscotched all over the park fishing the Firehole, the Gibbon, the Madison, the Gallatin, the Lamar, Slough Creek, the Lewis and others. We caught trophy-sized trout everywhere, keeping only those we needed for meals. In two weeks I ate more trout than in any similar time frame before or since. It was a wonderful experience, the highlight of which was our descent into Seven Mile Hole.

Seven mile Hole is in the rugged Yellowstone River canyon, between the upper and lower falls. It is reached by a trail of sorts from the Canyon Village Campground. Its name comes from the trail distance down to the bottom of the canyon.

It was a beautiful, bright, early summer morning full of bird song and emerging wildflowers when we started out, after first stashing a couple of beers in a shaded snow bank near the canyon rim. We probably made record time going down, running much of the way and taking shortcuts wherever possible.

Arriving at the bottom we were confronted by tons of turbulent, foam-topped green water hurling its bulk between and around massive boulders, some the size of a bungalow. At first glance the river here seemed unfishable, wading was certainly impossible. Careful checking soon revealed small pockets, runs and eddies where a weighted streamer or nymph could be maneuvered on a short line. One had to become a rock-hopper to fish these spots.

It was hard work but whenever we hooked a fish it was a good one. These were all native blackspotted cutthroat ranging from two to four pounds. You can imagine the trouble we had in bringing in a hooked trout from the heavy currents of that maelstrom. We lost many more than we landed but that really made little difference for we ended up keeping just one fish apiece. That's really all we wanted to tote up those steep return miles.

It took us four times longer to make it back up to the rim than it had to come down. I never tasted anything so refreshing as that can of beer dug out of the snow bank.

POOLS OF MEMORY

I n the two years following the end of my formal schooling I worked on a variety of jobs in the winter and spent the summers pursuing trout. During this time I fished waters all over the West, ranging from the mountain torrents of Glacier Park to Havasu Creek in the bottom of the Grand Canyon.

One of the most memorable of those expeditions was my quest for the lovely golden trout of the high Sierras. To get there I drove up the Owens River Valley to Bishop. Turning west, I took a trail road up Bishop Creek into the eastern foothills. The road terminated at a Forest Service horse camp. I parked the VW where it was pointed back down the grade and blocked the front wheels with large rocks, with the idea in mind that if the battery ran down during my absence I could get the car started by coasting downhill.

Shouldering my backpack containing food, a cooking kit, a change of clothes, sleeping bag and fishing tackle I set off up the slopes toward Bishop Pass, some 11,000 feet above. Late that afternoon I topped out over the rocky, treeless pass, walking across 20 foot banks of snow.

Once over the pass the going was easy and the trail one I could have followed in the dark. I camped that first night under the stars in the Palisade Basin beside a pair of small lakes, one of which furnished a brace of 10 inch brook trout for my evening meal.

The following day I hiked west until I hit the John Muir Trail, along the Middle Fork of the King's River. A Forest Service sign at this junction showed Simpson and Grouse Meadows to the south, with Big Pete and Little Pete Meadows to the north. I turned north. I was now in the heartland of this massive and magnificent range, surrounded on all sides by huge crags and spires of weather hewn granite. Their sheer sides were elaborately sculpted by eons of wind and water, frost and ice, with great snow-filled cirques and glaciated terraces. The air was so clear that all the peaks, even those most distant, appeared much closer than they were.

The Middle Fork of the King's River is a lovely, cascading

stream of moderate width. It shows itself here and there through the bankside groves of pine, hemlock and spruce in sun-bright riffles and small, flower spangled meadows.

I became so immersed in gazing at the grandeur surrounding me that I made little progress for an hour or two. The sheer, silent, forceful sense of isolation was joyful rather than ominous. I felt as though I were standing at the center of the universe with anything outside the encircling ranges being of little or no consequence.

My spellbound state was finally interrupted by the realization that I had reached the Little Pete Meadow stretch. Leaving my pack propped against the base of a large pine I assembled the little fly rod and reel, threaded the line and leader through the guides, tied on a size 14 Mosquito and, on hands and knees, crept to the grassy stream bank bordering a smooth run.

After couple of false casts to lengthen line, the fly dropped at the lower end of the incoming riffle. Almost as soon as the fly settled on the water a light streak flashed up from the depths and had it. After a short but spirited tug-of-war, I shortened the line and leader to a rod length and derricked the fish up onto the meadow grass beside me. My first golden trout and how gorgeous! He was only eight inches long but splendidly arrayed in a coat of gold and crimson with distinct underlying parr marks, orange-tipped dorsal fin, white-tipped anal and ventral fins and heavily spotted olive back and tail. The golden is undoubtedly the most beautiful of the trouts being surpassed in fresh water only by the Eastern brook trout which, although a *Salmonidae,* is actually a char rather than a trout.

Taking a fish on the first cast proved not to be any special

Lovely golden trout from Little Pete Meadows.

feat. It was obvious by their eagerness, and by the untrammeled and litter-free streambanks, that the area had not yet seen any fishing pressure. So long as one stayed out of sight, the goldens were ready takers of both dry flies and nymphs. I landed several more in fairly short order releasing all but the first and one other of the same size, which I kept for my evening meal.

Late in the afternoon I followed a game trail through open forest glades up the lower slopes bordering the eastern side of the valley. A couple thousand feet above the stream I hit a fairly flat, grassy bench on which was a tiny spring bordered by ferns, brook primrose and shooting stars: an ideal campsite, with a magnificent view. I stood quietly for some time looking far away through the granite peaks. It seemed I could see through to another dimension. It was all different, yet all the same—timeless and serene.

As I had no tent or tarp with me I set about constructing a simple lean-to, thatching the sides and roof with evergreen boughs, and set up a rock-rimmed fire pit in front of it. The little pan-fried goldens tasted as good as they looked having a delicate flavor that to my palate was much like that of westslope cutthroat. Under the lean-to I scooped out earth for under shoulder and hip positions, filled the hollows with pine needles and unrolled the down sleeping bag. As I settled in for the night, rattling rocks on the nearby game trail marked the progress of mule deer headed for the lush feed of the valley floor.

In the midsummer days that followed the weather, fortunately, remained mostly sunny and mild. I observed several thunder and lightning storms but they always seemed to occur at some distance from me. On only a couple of occasions was I forced to get under the canopy of a big pine or hemlock to escape a wetting. It was no trick to get under such cover in time for I could usually see the advancing curtain of rain while it was still some distance off. These high Sierra storms are violent but generally brief in duration.

Whenever leaning against the protection of a huge tree I always rubbed my hand gently over the rough trunk, hoping to absorb some of its strength and serenity. It is something I have done often since, and it works, because I believe it does.

I kept the side-hill aerie as base camp but spent many days wandering afield. I had a regional pocket map with me, obtained at McMurray's Sporting Goods in Bishop, and used it to find my way to small lakes and connecting streams designated as the home of golden trout. Sometimes I had rough trails to follow and sometimes I used cross-country dead reckoning. I found and fished the Treasure Lakes, Dusy Lakes, Desolation Lakes (a two day side trip) and others, unnamed, near Muir Pass.

The goldens I caught in these lakes were larger than their stream-based fellows but not quite so brilliant in coloring. I caught several of 17 and 18 inches but the average was 12 to 14 inches. As with brook trout, I felt size was of minor importance compared to the rare beauty of the fish and their fine taste.

Often the easiest method of ascent to the higher lakes was by hiking up the swiftly descending outlet streams. All of these watercourses, no matter of what volume, were home to a small, nondescript bird that has always been my favorite.

The ouzel (or dipper) is the talisman of tumbling waters, living wherever swift, clear water is found, from Alaska through Central America. The brownish-gray, thrush-sized ouzel has a way of life shared by no other bird. Its element is spray drenched boulders, from which it dives headfirst into the rushing currents and scrabbles about on the bottom in search of aquatic insect larvae. In doing so it uses its strong legs for clinging and its wings for added underwater balance and propulsion.

It was a never-ending source of amazement to watch him dive from his rock perch into a veritable torrent, certain to be swept far downstream immediately. Twenty to 30 seconds later he would pop up, like a cork from a champagne bottle, to light again on the very point of take-off.

Although not a relative its uptilted tail, bobbing stance and cheery burbling song might lead one to believe it is a water-dwelling wren. The ouzel builds a large circular nest of moss with a side entrance, choosing streamside rock crevices, overhangs or the spaces behind small waterfalls. It remains on even the far northern streams all year-round as long as the water remains open. Despite their bobbing, which looks like a nervous tic, they are calm and friendly little fellows and I never grew tired of sitting and watching quietly while one went about his business a few feet from me.

In those wanderings I came upon no camps, shacks, litter, hacked trees or other humans, with one fortuitous exception. I was actually on my way out, having run out of all food except trout, when I met a Forest Service wrangler leading a string of pack mules into the high country. During our trailside conversation I mentioned the fact that the only reason I was going out now was because I'd run out of staples.

"Well, hell, that's no problem," he replied. "I've got a bunch of extra grub I can give ya."

Newly fortified with beans, bacon, canned peaches and the makings for bannock I was able to extend the search for gold another glorious week.

When I finally came down out of those wild peaks, basins, meadows and tumbling streams it was with a distinct let-down feeling, as though I were leaving my real life behind me.

I must have a gene that orients me to mountains.

Addenda:

During the 1970s I read an article in a Sierra Club magazine that lamented the undiciplined incursion of mobs of "nature-loving" people into the high Sierra vastnesses. It described the John Muir Trail as being a veritable backpackers' highway, with as many as 200 weekend hikers camping on the shores of every easily accessible lake. It further detailed the resulting destruction of the delicate understory, the stream banks and other wildlife habitat, the overharvesting of fish, illegal tree cutting, open waste disposal and the painting of "John loves Mary" on granite boulders and cliff faces.

Will I ever go back again? I don't think so. I'd rather remember it as it once was.

Chapter 12
Wessel's Bend

I n the summer of 1952 I met Fred Bear, accompanying him on a western bow hunting trip, and was offered a job with his Bear Archery Company. The plant was located in Grayling, Michigan having been moved from Detroit in 1947.

In the spring of 1953 I met his daughter, Julia, and later that year we were married. Such was love that the ceremony took place during the height of the summer's largest river insect hatch. The event was further made notable by the organist who chose to play perhaps the only two pieces of music she knew well: "I'm Walking Behind You" and "How Much Is That Doggie In The Window?" Julia's two young children, Hannah and Christopher, showered us with rice as we emerged from the cool depths of the church.

Grayling was a small town of about 2,000 that had grown up during the white pine logging era of the mid nineteenth century. The main stream of the AuSable River flowed through the middle of town and wound its way, with adjoining branches, some two hundred miles to Lake Huron.

More than five billion board feet of white pine were floated down the AuSable (a French word meaning "River of Sands") during the several decades following the Civil War. Between 1867 and 1882 alone some 337 million board feet of timber were run down its branches.

Previous to the logging incursions the river had been both a travel route and food supplier to the Chippewa and Ottawa Indians. It was the habitat of a tremendous population of grayling, the beautiful fish noted for its sail-like dorsal fin and its excellent flesh. This member of the *Salmonidae* clan was less wary than most other game fish and was gregarious, gathering in huge schools over the main river channels.

By 1873 there was a railroad connecting the town with larger downstate metropolitan areas and weekend excursions poured into the region for its fishing. The town originally had been called Crawford but was renamed Grayling in 1874, in honor of the fish that gained it fame among visiting sportsmen.

Being unwary, avid feeders the grayling were subject to

destruction by overfishing. There were no limits imposed on the fishermen. Hundreds of grayling were caught daily with many left to rot on the river banks. This, plus the damage to the habitat by the loggers, sealed the fate of these lovely fish.

Log drives raked the mid stream spawning beds destroying eggs and fry. Ground bark from the logs, plus sand and silt from the log-gouged banks, covered the gravel beds and clogged the gills of adult fish. No longer shaded by the big pines, the river rose in temperature. By 1900 nearly all the grayling were gone. In 1908 the last officially recorded specimen was taken several miles below the town.

Rainbow trout had been planted in the AuSable around 1875 and brook trout had been introduced in 1885. The brookies got along very well. After the logging activity subsided and the grayling had been exterminated the river became increasingly important to the sportsmen of the state as a brook trout producer. Its fame spread, exceeding in popularity even the fabled rivers of northern Maine.

Humans learn slowly. The limit on brook trout was set at 50 with a six inch minimum size. By the time the European brown trout was introduced in 1891 the brookies were already sadly depleted and the ubiquitous browns rapidly took over as the most common and dominant fish.

This was the background of the great river system I resided near and came to know intimately. I had read somewhere that finding your own stretch of trout water is like finding your own woman and now was able to confirm this for myself. Basically they're all put together the same way but you become attached to a particular one for her individual topography. After you have lived with a few (stretches of water) you will be able to identify their subtle variations.

During the long spring to autumn seasons I was to be found somewhere on the AuSable nearly every evening. At one time or another I fished every stretch of the river from its headwaters above Frederic, Lovells and Roscommon, down through the big "Stillwaters" 30 miles below. The main stream (Middle Branch), the East Branch and the North Branch all offered a great variety of opportunities for the fly fisherman. Over the 26 years I lived there I gradually came to favor certain stretches of the South Branch and concentrated a great part of my efforts there.

The South Branch is the largest of the AuSable's courses. Between Roscommon and Smith Bridge there is a stretch of 14 miles of comparatively wild surroundings and perfect dry fly water. This land was deeded to the state by the late George Mason, with the provision that no more than the existing trail roads and no cabins or camps of any kind would ever be allowed. Other than the few dirt bush roads the only access is by canoe or

South Branch of the AuSable River. Wessel's Bend is in the background.

riverboat. The banks are heavily forested throughout with groves of red and Norway pine, maple, birch, beech, poplar, balsam and cedar and support a variety of wildlife, including many whitetail deer.

In addition to its surroundings the Mason Tract of the South Branch contained "heavier" water and greater mayfly hatches, resulting in larger sized trout, mostly browns, but also descendants of the older brook trout population.

One of my favorite South Branch spots was the area I called Wessel's Bend, as it was located just a bit upstream from the summer home of a friend, Madeline Wessels. The bend was a long L-shaped run, overhung along its outer contour by tag alders and sweepers. The AuSable sweepers are large cedars, undermined by the current until they topple into the water, cross-stream, anchored there by remaining root holds in the bank. When submerged in the water these cedar trunks never rot and form wonderful coverts for resting fish. My fondness for this stretch of water can be explained by the following entries in my field notes:

Saturday evening, June 19th, 1959: The "Michigan caddis" hatch (actually the large mayfly, *Hexagenia limbata)* had been on for a week on the mainstream. Fred Bear and I had experienced several good evenings just a mile or two downstream from Grayling, and had kept several nice browns up to three pounds for the freezer. The South Branch had been quiet that week—no caddis and no brown drakes. However, Saturday morning I had a call from Rosalynde Johnston. She had floated the Mason

53

Tract the evening before with Jerry McClane and reported that despite a severe thunderstorm she took some very nice fish and lost one of the largest she had ever hooked. She said both brown drakes and the big yellow caddis were in evidence.

I figured the next evening, after a hot, muggy day, it would be ripe there . . . but where to go? All the available access points would be mobbed with downstate hopefuls over the weekend. Then I thought of fairly secluded Wessell's Bend. It wasn't prime *Hexagenia* water, being mostly gravel bottom, but I had previously seen good brown drake flights there.

I drove in on the old grass-centered bush road by Madeline's, parked above a high sand bank, geared up, slid down the bank to the river and waded in. All was quiet except for the occasional zuu-oop of a diving nighthawk. It was then 9:20 p.m. I intended to wade across, then cut through the woods to a point a quarter of a mile above, which would give me a half mile of river to cover.

The hour surrounding sundown along such a river is magic. There is a brief period between dusk and full dark when the woods are hushed. Bird song and squirrel chatter are stilled, the only noticeable sound other than the nighthawks being the current's soft gurgling against my waders. It is the time when big bucks emerge from their secret daytime coverts and large trout slide out from under the jam piles and undercut banks to forage through their home pool and adjacent shallows.

I was halfway across the waist-deep run when suddenly, just 15 feet above me, I heard the slurp of a good fish. I hadn't seen any flies to that point but unhooked the Hatcher Caddis fly from the rod's keeper ring, pulled out about 10 more feet of line and made a tentative cast above the rise position. The fish took it on the first pass and ran strongly downstream . . . right between my legs! As you might guess, it is nearly impossible to step over a line or rod while waist deep in a strong current. I did about the only thing I could: passed the bowed rod, tip first, down between my legs and grabbed it behind me with the other hand. I then managed to turn around, all without becoming totally immersed. The fish was still on.

As I continued the battle I began to notice a few large flies floating by. *Hexes!* Then above me, up toward the corner bend, I heard more good fish begin feeding. I finally netted the 18 inch brown and wasted no time in continuing up to my intended starting point just above the L. As darkness fell the air cooled rather quickly and a heavy mist formed over the water. Fishing became largely a "by feel" process. I'd work down close to the sound of a feeding fish, then try to get the fly over his position and raise the rod tip when I heard him gulp. One out of every half dozen tries I'd be into a fish. Weird but strangely exciting.

My father-in-law, Fred Bear, preparing to try for an AuSable River brown.

Between 9:30 and 11:00 p.m. I took 14 fish, all 15 inches or better, on the deerhair bodied Hatcher Caddis pattern. I released all but the first fish which had taken the fly deeply behind the tongue and into the aorta. I had then used my hemostat to flatten the barb of the hook and had no trouble with the rest. The largest fish was just a shade over 20 inches.

When I got out of the river and climbed the bank to my car, the big yellow-bodied mayflies were still coming down from somewhere up above and fish were still noisily slurping under the alders and along the sweepers.

The next night, Sunday, I fished the same stretch. There were very few flies coming down but good fish were on the lookout for those that did. I took four respectable browns, all over three pounds, which were released. Tuesday night I was back again and there were fish feeding all over the river. I hooked one buster that got under a sweeper and broke the leader. A half hour later I connected with another dandy that I landed and released—22 inches and four and a half pounds. He had taken the fly so deeply that I cut off the tippet and left the fly in him rather than take the chance of causing him further damage. He wasn't bleeding so I assumed he'd recover. I took several more fish before 11:30, when the feeding spree slacked off. I finally climbed the sandy bank and struggled out of my waders. The man in the moon was grinning as I drove home.

Addenda:
Ten years after the 1978 move of the Bear Archery Company from Grayling to Gainesville, Florida my father-in-law and part-time fishing companion, Fred Bear, passed away. His ashes now repose along the bank of one of his favorite South Branch runs. If there are indeed souls I'm sure his is content in that lovely and peaceful place.

Chapter 13

Night Watch

Twenty miles downstream from the town of Grayling, at the head of the broad and deep Stillwaters where the South Branch merges with the AuSable Mainstream, lies a stretch called Connor's Flats. Much of this water is the type that must be waded with care as some of it is too deep or soft bottomed to cover on foot. One really familiar with the area can fish much of it by wading but it is largely water more suited to fishing from a canoe or boat.

No account of the AuSable River would be complete without some mention of the specialized boat developed there and bearing its name. The AuSable River Boat evolved during the early days of the lumbering industry as a modification of the Indians' dugout. There is no other river boat just like it anywhere. Ed Auger, a carpenter who lived in Grayling, is generally credited with its design.

The first ones built were 16 feet long. Later models, after 1890, were extended to either 22 or 24 feet. It is a narrow (20 to 24 inch beam) and shallow draft vessel, tapered at both ends. The angler in the front sits on a covered live well in which landed fish are kept during the day's float. The guide sits in the stern and guides the boat with a long pole or punt stick. A drag, usually of logging chain, slows the boat's forward rate to give the angler more time to cover lies back in above the sweepers and jam piles. The boat is so easy to steer that the guide or pusher can often fish and control the vessel's progress at the same time.

Originally the river boat was made of white pine or cedar and cost about $15. Modern models now use marine plywood coated with fiberglass or polyurethane and cost from several hundred to more than a thousand dollars.

At one time I was part owner of a fine, second-hand river boat, three of us having put in $25 each for its purchase. I didn't use it nearly as much as my companions, however, as I have always preferred the intimacy of wading in trout waters. It was very handy at times, though, especially in late June and early July when the big *Hexagenia* and brown drake hatches occurred in the Stillwaters. The three of us would put the river boat in near Wakeley Bridge at dusk and float down into Connor's Flats. Near

The AuSable riverboat in action.

the mouth of the South Branch I would get out of the boat and fish by wading, while my companions went further downstream.

This big water has long been noted for its lunker browns. These fish are largely night feeders, keeping under cover during the hours when most fishermen are on the river. It is mostly mud bottom, producing tremendous numbers of the big burrowing mayfly nymphs *(Hexagenia* and *Ephemera).*

By the time I eased into the river currents it was usually dark and the big flies would be starting to hatch, as evidenced by the loud slurps of avidly feeding trout. By the time my friends had poled the boat back up to where I was stationed (around mid night) we had all normally experienced several great battles with browns measured in pounds rather than inches.

The most unforgettable memory I have of Connor's Flats was the night I got cleaned. I was standing in a broad and deep reach of water, nearly to the top of my waders. Twenty feet in front of me, under a big overhanging birch, was a monstrous trout I had located the previous night. Every time the fish rose I could plainly feel the wash of water that threatened to flow over the rim of my waders. I was casting by feel (it was too dark to see the rises) but the noise made by the fish was locator enough.

Finally, after several dozen floats, the great trout sucked in my *Hex* fly and turned downstream with a rush when I struck back. I could neither stop nor slow him. He peeled all the line from my reel and I was left sadder but wiser sans line, leader, fly and fish.

Browns of nearly 20 pounds have been taken from this water. I'd love to know how big that particular fish was. It marked

Fishing after dark during a heavy hatch is a whole new ball game.

the only time in my experience I've had that happen and it taught me a lesson. After that I began filling my reels with plenty of backing under the fly line.

Following the period of the big after-dark hatches the species of aquatic insects emerging through the remainder of the summer are generally very tiny, needing delicate leader tippets and size 20 or smaller flies to fool the trout. A great many fishermen give up during this period, feeling that the extra effort is either too involved or just not worth the trouble. The big fish are still there and as the pressure slackens the fishing becomes both more challenging and pleasurable. Not only is this true of the tiny mayfly hatches of early morning and late evening but also during the darker hours when the lunker browns abandon their daytime caution and cruise out into open and often shallow water to feed on crayfish and minnows.

Most fishermen are nervous about wading at night, either because they are not familiar enough with their surroundings or because they just feel uneasy in the dark. I came to thoroughly enjoy the quiet and peaceful night watch having been introduced to its mysteries by "Sailor Bill" Huddleston, a commercial fly tier and seeker of big trout. His revamped school bus was a summer fixture for many years near the mid-Grayling river crossing.

The big key to night fishing is to become intimately familiar with the stretch of water to be fished so you will know all the details of depth, currents, overhanging brush, jam piles, sunken logs and limbs, etc. This is because you will be fishing largely by feel rather than by sight, and errors in footwork can require a soggy retreat. The section of stream you choose is more important than the stream itself. I always keep an eye out for deep water bends, log jams, stumps with roots attached and riffles shelving into a deep hole. When fishing the river during the day I mentally marked the location of large pools that really looked "hot" but produced no action, this often being an indicator of large resident trout having consumed or driven out all lesser fish.

Connor's Flats seemed to me to offer the most likely set of conditions for night work and I was seldom disappointed. I preferred warm, muggy nights during the dark phase of the moon— the darker the better. Armed with my favorite rod, floating line, seven feet of 1X leader and a size 4X or 6X black and white bucktail, I'd cast across stream or quartering slightly upstream and let the fly swing around in a dead drift. A fish might hit the bucktail anytime during its drift but did so most often just as it was arcing around near the end of its swing.

Patience is the second key to night fishing. Big fish are continually cruising and it is often some time before a resident comes in contact with your offering. I have cast repeatedly through the same pool or run 30 or 40 times with the next drift resulting in all hell breaking loose. Two or three pools or bends are about all I'd cover in three to four hours fishing.

When a big trout takes at night it is usually a vicious strike. I've actually had the rod torn from my grasp by a sudden tremendous smash.

On occasion, large, dark colored, bushy dry flies tied with deer or elk hair to insure good flotation worked well, as would a deer hair mouse and even a bass-sized popping bug. When fishing on the surface it was more effective to impart some action to the fly or lure rather than let it dead drift.

Since moving away from the AuSable I've used the night watch in many other rivers, both in North America and abroad, with worthwhile results. It works everywhere there are lunker trout. In many areas of Argentina, Chile, New Zealand and Tasmania night fishing is the most popular method among experienced fly anglers and many of their favored locations are lake inlets and stream outlets.

Addenda:
Hundreds of homesites and summer cottages have consumed much of the AuSable's forested banks, many owners clearing out trees and undergrowth in favor of expansive lawns.

Grayling is just a tank of gas away from the urban sprawls of

Detroit, Ann Arbor, Lansing, et al, and fishing pressure has increased exponentially to the point where the public stretches are usually overcrowded during summer weekends. Because of the pressure much of the fishing is now restricted to catch-and-release. Many of the river's once heavy fly hatches have dwindled. Others remain largely intact.

Due to seemingly unstoppable littering problems many of the river frontage dwellers will not allow foot passage through their property. There are a number of public landings offering access to waders and boats but these are miles apart and suffer very heavy traffic. The only way to cover many stretches of the river is by canoe or river boat and this has led to an even larger problem so far as the fishing is concerned.

In the 1930s there was one canoe livery in Grayling. By 1970 five liveries were in operation with over a thousand canoes on the river every Saturday and Sunday. Additional canoe liveries in Roscommon on the South Branch added to the melee. The great bulk of canoeists are urban folk out for a weekend vacation. Most are not ecologically aware. Regardless of various schemes to limit it, littering in and on the banks of the river remains a severe problem.

Despite these drawbacks the AuSable still retains its sparkling appeal, having thus far endured all the ravages of advancing civilization. It will never be what it was, even a quarter century ago, but it lives on and still produces modest numbers of good fish.

Chapter 14
Corral Creek Run

T he year, 1960. The time, midSeptember. The place, central British Columbia, the Kispiox River valley 50 miles north of Hazelton. The party, Fred Bear and I, with a bow hunt for grizzlies uppermost in mind plus Knick Knickerbocker of Crozet, Virginia and George Griffith of Grayling, Michigan who were along to tangle with the great migrant steelhead of the region.

We were headquartered at Jack Lee's cabin camp, where Corral Creek runs into the Kispiox. Jack had driven us in from our air arrival point at Smithers, over a gravel road that was fairly good going out of Hazelton but that gradually downgraded to bush road status as we progressed up the wide, forested valley. At one point we crossed a wooden bridge spanning a deep stream cleft. The rough sign at the bridge proclaimed this to be "Nobody Much Creek." When Fred asked Jack how it got that name, the outfitter replied, "Well, before the bridge was put in, nobody much got beyond that spot in a car."

Jack, incidentally, was a remnant of a now vanishing breed, hard working and self sufficient pioneer stock. He was intimately familiar with the surrounding wilderness, largely the result of a rough winter during the Great Depression of the 1930s when he had taken to the forest with nothing but snowshoes, bedroll, a single shot .22 rifle and some salt. He hunted red squirrels for their pelts, which at the time were worth 10 cents apiece, and lived largely on the small carcasses of his quarry. It was a time of constant travel, walking along looking for a new target while skinning with his pocket knife the last one taken. By the time he came out in the spring, Jack had bagged more than 3,000 squirrels and in the process had become familiar with every nook and cranny he would later take over as a guiding territory.

At that time this north central wilderness of British Columbia was a land of primeval beauty, lushly forested with huge spruce and fir, dotted with innumerable lakes and crisscrossed by the valleys and gorges of such mighty river systems as the Nass, Nelson, Dease and Skeena.

The great Skeena watershed system rises in the heart of the interior Stikine, Skeena and Omineca ranges and fed by sizable tributaries such as the Bulkley, Babine, Morice, Sustut, Copper and Kispiox, winds its way 500 miles to the Pacific south of Prince Rupert.

North of Hazelton the timbered mountains stretched out in wild profusion for 300 miles, for the most part unmarred by human habitation but supporting a wealth of mountain sheep and mountain goats, moose, caribou, wolves and bears, both black and grizzly. Outfitters' pack strings periodically penetrated some of the more accessible portions of this area but most of the country remained aloof and pristine.

In terms of both number and size of fish the Skeena system has long been the world's top producer of steelhead. The steelhead is an anadromous strain of the rainbow trout. It is one of the world's truly great fresh water game fish; in fighting qualities the Pacific Ocean's equivalent to the Atlantic's *Salmo salar*. In general habits and life history the steelhead is also close to the Atlantic salmon, the one big exception is that he feeds while in fresh water.

For many years it was thought the steelhead would not take flies, an unfortunate belief that downgraded their reputation as a game fish and, because commercial fishing was given priority over sportfishing, led to unnecessary depletion of the stock. Steelhead (named for the hardness of the bone structure in the skull) are hereditary in their sea-running cycle and their spawning runs up into the interior rivers take place largely in September and October.

While Fred and I were attempting to encounter one of the region's grizzlies, George and Knick had taken several fine steelhead on light spinning tackle, the fish ranging from 12 to 17 pounds and had hooked and lost even larger ones. They reported the river full of fish, which sorely tested my bow hunting determination.

I did take one midday hike to nearby Skunsnat Lake, where I managed to catch enough one to three pound cutthroat trout to feed our group that evening. A rubber raft Jack had cached on the lake shore and the uneducated and eager trout combined to make it a relaxed and pleasurable change of pace.

Then, two days before the end of our stay, I had the thrill of a successful encounter with a grizzly, one of the first to be taken in modern times with the bow and broadhead arrow. My luck was really at its height, for this left me with time enough to give the Kispiox steelhead a try. I wasted no time taking advantage of it.

Early the following morning I jointed my fly rod, attached a new eight pound test leader to the line, tied on a size 6 Skykomish Sunrise fly and headed for the river. The Corral Creek cabins were situated on a high bank overlooking the river, 200 yards below. To get there all I had to do was step out the front door and half-skid, half-stumble, down the steep blackberry-thicketed slope to the

Kispiox River steelhead, taken from the run shown in the background.

river's edge, then walk up to where it shallowed enough to permit a cautious thigh-deep crossing. Below the tumbling riffles of the crossing, and on the camp side of the river, was a smooth, waist-deep run, a hundred yards in length, tailing out in another boulder-strewn riffle before entering a huge jam-piled U bend where Corral Creek entered. The run appeared to be an ideal holding area for steelhead.

The morning was dull and overcast which is why I had chosen the Skykomish Sunrise. I had previously found fish to be more selective about fly patterns on such a day, perhaps because the colors of flies are less distinct from below in bright light and more easily seen in weak light. I used the same greased line method that I prefer for Atlantic salmon. Casting the floating line up and across-stream I let the wet fly dead drift about six inches under the surface as it swung down and eventually across the midrun currents, mending line as necessary to prevent undue drag.

I had systematically fished down nearly the entire run with no sign of a fish. As the swimming fly arced across the hastening current just upstream of the outlet riffle, the forward progress of line and fly stopped short and I instinctively reared back in a hard strike. A huge boil welled to the surface and the Hardy reel began its fitful song.

During the ensuing struggle I was very fortunate that the fish chose to stay in the long run. If he had turned downstream through the boulders and into the 15 foot depths under the jam piles, I doubt that I could have held him. At one point the line suddenly slackened as he turned toward me. I frantically stripped in line but was unable to match the fish's speed. When I managed to tighten up the line once more I was considerably relieved to find him still hooked.

For a half hour the steelhead took advantage of the long line and heavy current to fight deep and strong. He did not jump or porpoise and I had no sight of him until the very end, as he slowly came into the gravelly shallows, his curved jaw open and the fly showing bright in the angle of his jaw. Lord, he was big! A magnificent fresh run male fish, perfectly formed and highly colored, he weighed in at 26 1/2 pounds. Stuffed and baked by Jack's wife, Francis, it was the basis of a memorable meal.

Addenda:

Steelhead runs in the great tributaries of the Skeena watershed are presently all endangered due to a combination of overexploitation by commercial salmon fishermen, Indians, sport fishermen and riverine habitat destruction through clearcut logging and road building. There is now a new, improved highway up the length of the Kispiox valley. Grizzlies are gone from the area where we hunted, having been forced farther north into the mountains by human encroachment.

Forest cover in the high hills is the basic protector of game fish waters. The clearcutting of timber as presently being practiced both on the Pacific slopes and inland watersheds is immensely destructive. It removes the shade and soil-holding ability of the watersheds causing siltation of spawning-beds, warming water temperature, winter floods and summer droughts.

The Skeena has been exploited as a commercial salmon fishery since the late 1800s. The Department of Fisheries in British Columbia estimates that 50 percent of the steelhead runs are depleted in this process through purse seining and gill netting in the Pacific estuaries.

Commercial fishermen seem to think that hatcheries are the answer to dwindling anadromous fish stocks. Up to now, a proliferation of west coast hatcheries has caused more problems than they've solved. Modern runs are a fraction of historic runs. It has been shown that of more than three million young hatchery raised steelhead dumped into Pacific feeders, fewer than one in 300 ever returns as an adult.

It took a collapse of the Atlantic salmon fishery in the Northeast before any real action was taken to limit the catch and to protect the habitat. Such history will probably be repeated concerning the anadromous stocks of the Northwest. It is one thing to voice concern, quite another to instigate proper controls. For here, as in every conservation issue where vested interests are concerned, the powerful, monied exploiters always seem to win which means, in the end, we all lose.

Chapter 15
Sutton Salters

I n his capacity as head of the Fisheries Division of the Michigan Department of Conservation, Wayne Tody had contacted his counterpart at the Ontario Department of Lands & Forests for information on what they considered to be the best brook trout fishing in their province.

Ontario has long been noted for its wealth of squaretail habitat but the answer Wayne received was unequivocal—the Sutton River in August. As the Ontario official expressed it, "When the sea trout run in, adjectives run out!"

Wayne and fisheries co-worker Troy Yoder promptly made plans for a small expedition to include four of the Conservation Department's regional wardens, who also happened to be dedicated anglers.

Among the latter was Clarence Roberts, a game and fish warden headquartered in Grayling. Clarence was a large man, well over six feet and two hundred pounds. He was an excellent woodsman and angler. Despite his huge hands, which were twice the size of mine, he was the finest dry fly tier I have ever known.

I had come to know Clarence quite well although his professional duties prevented us from sharing many outings. On the occasion in question one member of the original party had to cancel out because of illness in his family and Wayne had asked Clarence to choose a substitute.

"Would you like to go?" Clarence asked me.

"Would a cow lick Lot's wife?" I quickly replied.

On August 5, 1963 our small group took off in two vehicles from Michigan's Upper Peninsula, across the bridge at Sault Ste. Marie, to the Trans-Canada Highway then west along the north shore of Lake Superior to White River.

Advance arrangements had been made with the White River Air Service to fly us to Hawley Lake, headwaters of the Sutton River.

One and a half hours after our 7:30 a.m. take-off the Otter set down on Portage Lake for refueling. We continued on north across miles of tundra and stunted spruce, crisscrossed at intervals by the Kenogami, Little Current, Attawapisket and Ekwan river systems. We had one other enforced two hour layover on Percy

Lake while we waited for a low ceiling to clear.

Finally arriving at Hawley Lake in mid afternoon, we taxied to the Cree village just above the river outlet. The village population was 40, most of whom were related members of three family groups. The Chookomolin brothers, Eli and Little Joe, were the head men.

Our cabin accommodations were small but clean and adequately comfortable. After unpacking and getting gear squared away we spent the evening trolling for lake trout (Mackinaw), taking six on trolled T-spoons.

Most of the following day was also spent on Hawley Lake although in the afternoon Clarence and I canoed down the out-flowing river four or five miles to the first rapids, where we caught enough brookies for a camp meal. We took these 18 to 20 inch fish on Mickey Finn streamers.

On August 7 our entire party, consisting of Wayne Tody, Troy Yoder, Roger Wood, Don Zettle, Clarence Roberts, our Indian guides and myself, took off downriver in three large Chestnut freighter canoes. The combination of two anglers and one guide in each of the 20 foot canoes was ideal both for traveling and for fishing. Our Cree guides, Onesime Wheesk, Joe Spence and Eli Metat proved to be efficient, easy-going and amiable although quite reserved in nature.

Stopping at intervals to fish, we cruised down the river for

Early morning preparations on Ontario's Sutton River.

16 miles before reaching a tent camp set up previously by the guides on a large horseshoe bend. Clarence and I were the only die-hard fly fishermen in our party, the others using lightweight spinning gear. Troy intended to keep an exact record of fish

caught and had asked each of us to keep close tabs on how many trout we landed, as all but what we needed for meals were to be released. Between the lake and the camp we took more than a hundred large brookies, averaging 18 inches and three to three and a half pounds, nine of which we kept for a streamside lunch.

The large 16 by 20 foot wall tent in which we slept was outfitted with light spring frames on spruce pole bunks, over which we spread our down bags. The Cree slept in a smaller tent a few yards away.

Breakfasts here were never too early, nor dinners too late, to discourage the presence of the north country's camp followers, the Whiskey Jacks or Canadian Jays. The Crees believe these small gray ghosts, as quiet on the wing as an owl, contain the souls of lost trappers and voyageurs. Therefore, they will never harm them even in the harshest winter when anything else, large or small, is a possibility for the cooking pot. These birds in turn are very friendly little fellows and have an unbelievable appetite, gorging all the handouts of meat or bread that are offered. After a day or two in one location one can have them taking scraps from the hand.

For the following four days we ranged up and down the Sutton finding its clean, gravelly beds absolutely filled with brookies. Many of these fish were fresh-run from Hudson Bay and were quite silvery in overall color, lacking the bright patterning they would gradually assume after a week or two in fresh water. Such sea-run brook trout are called salters by the Canadians. They are tremendous fighters and their dark red flesh is a gourmet's delight.

The guides usually arranged it so that although scattered while fishing they'd head the canoes to a prearranged location at noon for a group shore lunch. They carried a large square skillet on which the filleted trout were cooked, along with bacon and fried potatoes. Other pots over the dead spruce wood fire heated beans and coffee.

Once we were stuffed a short siesta was in order while our guides cleaned up. I was highly impressed with the way they did this. By the time we embarked for more fishing you could not tell that anyone had been there. They buried all traces of the drowned fire, even including the chips from the spruce used as fuel, beneath the heavy ground carpet of reindeer moss. I noticed too that they discarded nothing in the river and kept the campsite spotlessly clean.

From Hawley Lake it is 80 miles by river to Hudson Bay. We fished some 30 miles of this distance, going downstream another 14 miles below our tent camp. We were fortunate during our stay to have decent weather. The temperature went down to freezing at night. Days were mostly sunny and cool with a few light intermittent rain squalls.

Smaller forms of life were constantly encountered: mink, beaver, otter, muskrat, osprey, broad-winged hawks, ravens, black ducks, green winged teal, greater and lesser yellowlegs, the Canada jays and many others. Every pool, bend, run and rapid held its quota of salters. I have never before or since experienced a river so filled with fish. In four days our combined tally added up to 500 trout. Figuring a very conservative estimate of a two and a half pound average, we caught well over a half ton of brook trout!

The most notable occurrence from my viewpoint happened

Clarence Roberts with an average Sutton River squaretail.

on our second day in camp. Clarence and I convinced our guide that we should backtrack upriver a couple miles to a beautiful stretch of boulder-studded rapids and pocket water. Once there we beached the canoe and, while our guide looked for blueberries, fished by wading. We hadn't been there long when I began to notice huge sink-size rises. Looking more closely at the surface I soon spotted big mayflies bobbing along like miniature sailboats. They were our old friends, the Michigan "caddis." I previously had no idea they ranged this far north (I later found them even further north on the rivers of Quebec and Labrador). Both Clarence and I had imitations in our fly boxes and wasted no time

70

in switching to them. I have never elsewhere experienced such savage surface rises as these salters made. They hit our flies with total abandon, creating about as much turmoil as if a large dog had jumped in the river. We took several trout there over 20 inches in length and between four and five pounds in weight. Incredibly productive fishing.

The day before we returned to the Hawley Lake Village for our flight out we each saved 10 fish, which the Cree smoked for us overnight in a home-made willow frame smokehouse. I've never seen anything disappear so fast as a plate of this smoked brook trout later set out as appetizers at a home dinner party.

Chapter 16

Hola Pescadore

The mid 1960s proved to be a period of transition for me. One summer evening, due to a misunderstanding between an automobile, a soft gravel shoulder, several large pines and myself, I was brought into the Grayling hospital no longer possessing the bilateral symmetry which I had originally been issued.

After a couple of years in and out of hospitals and three pelvic operations later I was finally turned loose on the world again, handicapped somewhat by crutches, which the doctors doubted I'd ever do without.

During the abundance of time I'd had to think about it, I'd decided that there were places I wanted to see and things I wanted to do that I'd better take care of before anything else drastic happened.

In particular, I'd decided that I must see and fish the Patagonian wilderness. This desire had actually begun three years previously when a friend, Mort Neff of the "Michigan Outdoors" television series, related almost unbelievable tales of the incredible fishing to be had in that wild frontier far below the equator. One of his accounts in particular, that of watersheds holding only huge Eastern brook trout, had been the determining convincer.

Prior to my crack-up I had actually begun a correspondence with one of Mort's contacts, a Mrs. Ruth Haessler, who with her son, Raul San Martin, ran a guiding service from the village of Esquel, Argentina. I now wrote them again and made final arrangements.

The following March of 1966, having put both my job and my marriage on hold, I flew from my Michigan home to Miami and 24 hours later, after stops in Panama City, Lima, Peru and Santiago, Chile the Pan Am jet liner coasted to a landing 8,000 miles from my starting point in Buenos Aires. Transferring to Aerolineas Argentinas, and after another 2,000 miles southwest, the twin engine Caravelle landed at Esquel, literally the end of the line.

Upon meeting Mrs. Haessler I found that her son, Raul, was overdue in returning from a compulsory term of service with the army. So I spent the ensuing week with Carlos, a young friend of

Raul's, as guide, fishing the various streams flowing into and connecting Lagos Futalaufquen, Verde, Krueger, Situacion and Menendez. The fish we took were all rainbows, or Arco iris as the South Americans call them, ranging from two to six pounds. We also fished the Rio Frey that, in addition to rainbows, has a healthy population of landlocked salmon averaging nine to 10 pounds in weight and wilder fighters, to my mind, than the Arco iris.

Wading the swift river currents with crutches was difficult but by taking it slowly I made out all right, becoming totally immersed only once. Fortunately the river bottoms in that region were mostly of sand and gravel, with few boulder-strewn stretches. Because my mobility was limited, the larger fish often had me well down into my fly line backing. I mainly used small streamers and nymphs and seldom had to cast a dozen times between strikes.

At the end of the week Raul returned from his army stint, and after a day spent getting his Jeep station wagon and outboard motor tuned up and buying supplies, we took off one sunny morning, bound for Lago General Paz, 300 kilometers to the south.

I should mention that this Patagonian region comprises some 311,000 square miles of southern Argentina and Chile, extending from the Limay and Rio Negro watersheds at latitude 40 degrees south to the Straits of Magellan. The bulk of this vast territory, lying in Argentina east of the Andes, consists of dry, brown prairie land called pampas, vegetated mainly with coarse grasses and open scrub. Its starkness is broken here and there by huge sheep and cattle ranches or estancias. The Chilean portion of Patagonia is utterly different. Most of it is mountainous and uninhabited, a region of tempest and torrential rains, containing fantastically beautiful geographic forms including a labyrinth of coastal fjords, extensive glaciation, dense subtropical forests and mountain massifs.

The few Patagonian roads are rough at best, and towing a 20-foot boat on a trailer, it took us 10 hours to negotiate the 180 miles, including a lunch stop in the small pampas village of Tecka. The last 36 kilometers from Rio Pico found us winding up into the mountains through dense forests of linga and coihue trees. The track ended at Vintter, a tiny settlement high on the slopes above Lago General Paz.

Insofar as angling is the interest many of the Argentine lakes extend deep into the heart of the cordillera, often with their headwaters in Chilean territory. Lago General Paz (called Lago Vintter on some maps) is among these nationally divided watersheds. It lies in an east/west orientation at an elevation of 1,500 feet and is some 50 miles in length. The western third of the lake is in Chile and the Chileans call it Lago Palena. Its outlet, the Rio Corcovado, flows out of the Argentine end but curves around through a deep pass into Chile and eventually, as Rio Palena, empties into the Gulfo Corcovado on the Pacific side.

After a night spent in an unoccupied cabin in Vintter we maneuvered the car and trailer down to the lake shore and launched our boat. A two hour cruise up the lake brought us to the only inhabited spot on its expanse, a Chilean border police post on the northern shore. There has always existed considerable controversy between the two countries over the boundary and at intervals such guard posts are maintained, ostensibly to prevent unauthorized ingress and smuggling.

Although I had purchased a Chilean fishing license we felt it

Six and seven pound brook trout caught in Lago Palena, Chile.

best to check in with the guards and try to establish friendly relations so that our comings and goings on the lake would not be suspect. However, we found the post deserted. One of the crude cabins had a gas barrel stove and a large supply of firewood so we forgot about pitching our tent and became cabin squatters. Violent wind and rain storms sweeping down from the towering Andes are common here and the cabin afforded added shelter from such an occurrence.

The next six days are a time I can never forget. Raul and I traveled all over the Chilean end of the lake, beaching our boat near the mouths of streams entering from glacial cirques many thousands of feet above, then wading along the drop-offs and casting our sinking lines and flies into the depths.

This watershed contains only Eastern brook trout, descendants of eggs and fry shipped to Argentina from Maine in the early 1900s. Our first beachhead was near a crystalline stream emerging abruptly from the forest canopy into a deep current-cut inlet channel.

Because of my crutches it took me a little longer to get rigged up and into a favorable casting position. I had just begun to lay out line when a great shout arose from Raul, accompanied by the whine of his reel. His rod was bent over in a full arc and dancing madly as something in the depths stripped line through the guides. "Wow!" I thought, "Sure hope there are more like that around!"

I had momentarily ceased my retrieve while watching Raul but I had no sooner drawn in the slack line when a tremendous strike nearly tore the rod from my hand. Whatever I was fast to was a heavyweight! I returned Raul's joyful shout before concentrating fully on the business at hand. The fish fought deep and strong with many savage heart-stopping head shakes.

I'm not sure how long it was before I felt any weakening of

A ten pound squaretail taken at the boca of the Pichi Traful.

its strength but suddenly the water welled up as the great trout surfaced. The sight of that "canoe paddle" side, white-edged fins and big square tail as it rolled was breathtaking. I had often dreamed of catching a brook trout of those dimensions but now that the dream was near reality my shaking legs threatened to give way. I did, though, slowly force the big squaretail into the shallows and the battle was won. Life occasionally provides moments of complete happiness. This, for me, was one.

That brook trout was 22 inches long, 17 in girth, and the pointer of the little Chatillon scale didn't stop until it was well over the six pound mark. Incredible! Raul's trout was a half pound heavier. Better was to come.

The waters of Lago Palena are an intense cobalt blue and so clear you can see every pebble on the bottom, 20 feet down. The color is so deeply magnetic that it tightens the stomach muscles and slows the breathing. Gazing over the side of the boat while traveling between stream mouths I had the unearthly sensation of my soul being drawn into its depths.

Sandy shorelines near the stream inlets bore no marks of human presence save our own. No tin cans, bottles or other debris were there—only the prints of puma, huemal and wild boar. There is a strange feel about the surrounding Patagonian forest, eerie but not unfriendly, as though it belonged to another geological age. Birds were everywhere, from tiny jewel-plumaged hummingbirds to giant Andean condors riding the thermals high above the mountain spires, so high that to look at them hurt the eyes. The forest edge seemed alive with teru terus, bandurrias, tercels, green parrots and the sparrow-sized chucao which calls its name in a voice that seems like it would have to come from a bird many times the size of this little fellow.

In the days that followed we fished a half dozen stream inlets hooking into scores of big brook trout, releasing all but the few we saved for the table. In all that time we caught only one fish of less than four pounds in weight. Our largest pair topped eight pounds. We know that even bigger ones dwell there. I hooked, fought and finally lost a fish that both Raul and I guessed would top 10 pounds. The fly pulled out just as I was bringing him into the shallows. Raul's father had previously taken one of 15 pounds from this lake.

Their flesh was fire-red and delectable, the result of a diet that included a small fresh water crab called cangrejo in Argentina and pancora in Chile. The rivers and lakes are full of these quarter-sized crustaceans. Our most successful fly patterns were of the Woolly Worm type; yellow body with brown palmered hackle and black body with yellow-dyed gray hackle and two South American patterns, the Campeone (red tail, green wool body with small white butt and silver rib, heavy wing of peacock herl, overlaying shoulders of teal flank feather, dark red hackle and red head) and the Matona (Lady Killer) which is a simple but effective pattern having no tail or body, just a short streamer wing of yellow-dyed grizzly hackles and the same feather wound on as hackle and flared back around the hook shank.

In addition to the small crustaceans there are a few species of

A predominantly crustacean diet makes the flesh of Patagonian brook trout bright red— and delicious.

small forage fishes, fresh water shrimp and aquatic insects such as caddis, mayflies and stoneflies although these are not as prominent as in many of our North American rivers. Rainbows and brown trout are often taken with dry flies, while wet patterns are generally more effective for the brookies and landlocks.

Wherever you go in Patagonia and whatever species of game fish you prefer—rainbows, browns, brook trout or landlocked salmon—your chances of hooking into many large fish are greater than in any other earthly region I know of.

Chapter 17
Off The Track

New Zealand, which has long enjoyed a unique reputation for the variety and challenge of its game fishing, was on my list of places to visit.

Brown trout ova introduced from England via Tasmania were first successfully hatched there in 1867. Rainbow trout spawn from the Russian River in California were hatched in 1883. Both species bred prolifically and were stocked throughout the country, thriving in its insect-rich, cold, clear lakes and thousands of miles of rivers and streams.

New Zealand is made up of two main islands. On the North Island are the lake systems of Taupo and Rotorua which in themselves have given the country a reputation for superb angling. Brown trout are plentiful in this area but are greatly outnumbered by the rainbows. The Tongariro River, a major feeder of Lake Taupo, gained fame largely through the writings of Zane Grey who tested its waters.

The South Island is 750 miles long by road and averages 150 miles in width. The Southern Alps, with Mounts Cook and Tasman as dominant features, form a backbone throughout its length. Snow melt from the glaciers nourishes all the earth below on its journey to the Tasman and South Pacific seas. Brown trout predominate in these waters but there are also rainbows and land-locked salmon in many of its lakes and rivers.

In midFebruary of 1969 I drove from Michigan to Los Angeles, sold my car, got my passport renewed and boarded a plane bound for the land down under. By this time I had graduated from crutches to a cane, considerably improving my mobility.

After a short stop in Papeete I arrived in New Zealand's largest city, Auckland, at noon of the following day. It was windy and raining lightly but not cold, the temperature being in the 60s.

Upon clearing customs I found a car rental agency and rented a new Austin Mini, a vehicle just large enough to hold my luggage and me. The fee for a month's rental and 3,000 miles, including insurance, was $250 which I considered extremely reasonable, especially since the tiny sedan covered 45 miles on a gallon of gas.

I had to start out from the center of the city, cold turkey, driving for the first time in the left hand lane. It was nerve-wracking until I got out of city traffic. The New Zealand highways are well-surfaced but are narrow at two lanes.

Kiwi drivers seem to have copied their style from those on the Los Angeles freeway, driving everywhere at top speed. Coming up behind you on a stretch of road where they can't pass they tailgate until they can get by, a custom I find uncomfortable. On the hilly roads they usually drive over the center line and on several occasions I experienced near-misses with oncoming traffic. My luck held out and the only trouble I experienced during my entire stay was one flat tire.

I spent the first day sightseeing along the northern coast and becoming acclimated to the unfamiliar driving style. My first fishing stop was in Rotorua. I spent over a week in that general area, fishing the streams entering lakes Rotorua and Tarawera and the Kaituna River between lakes Rotorua and Rotoiti.

Fishing the mouth of Holden's Bay Stream one evening on Lake Rotorua I met a resident fisherman, Wally Jensen, whom I later discovered was locally famous for his angling exploits. Wally was a self-sufficient widower, tall, lean and rather taciturn. He had a large, well-furnished home not far from the lake and was a passable cook. We struck up a friendship and he invited me to stay with him, which I did for several days. During that period we not only waded the rivers during morning and evening sessions but did some midday trolling from Wally's small outboard boat on the lakes. For this we used our fly rods, paying out 30 or 40 yards of line in the wake of the rowed boat and using local streamer fly patterns such as the Mrs. Simpson or Parson's Glory, tied to represent small fresh water smelt.

I didn't really keep score but between us we daily caught a dozen or more rainbows of three to six pounds. These were run-of-the-mill fish for that area. Wally showed me the mount of a 23 1/2 pound trout and one in his freezer of 14 pounds, both from Lake Tarawera. It must be added that fish that large are not numerous.

We also fished after dark in the mouths of streams entering the lakes. These sessions were for cruising trout, using a sinking tip line and streamers, and the fishing pace was slower but nearly always productive with a good fish or two. In the Ngongataha River mouth on Rotorua and the Orchard Stream mouth on Tarawera, we took several rainbows of five and six pounds (estimated weights—I did not have a scale with me). This night fishing is popular throughout New Zealand and accounts for most of the larger trout taken.

I found here, as in the rest of that country, that although some of my North American nymph patterns such as the Gold Ribbed Hare's Ear, the March Brown and the Olive Sedge worked well, for dry fly or streamer use the New Zealand patterns seemed to produce the best. Among these are the Kakahi Queen, Twilight Beauty, Dad's Favorite and Cock-y-bondu in sizes 12 and 14 for dry fly work and the Hairy Dog, Scotch Poacher, Hamill Killer and Parson's Glory for streamer fishing.

During our drives to reach angling spots, and later in the fjordland regions of the South Island, I discovered that New Zealand has a primeval beauty not readily discernible from the main highways. One needs to get off on the side tracks to encounter the dawn world aspect of exotic pine, acacia and eucalyptus forests with giant tree ferns and colorful bird life. The majority of its running waters are glass-clear and, like Scotland, it has an amazing amount of wild unsettled stretches in proportion to its relatively small overall size.

From Rotorua I drove to Taupo which is near the center of the North Island. Wally had called a friend, Bob Sullivan, who ran

Tieke Falls pool on the Waihaha River, a feeder of Lake Taupo.

a Sporting Goods Store there, as an introduction to my visit. Bob was also an enthusiastic angler and had spent years exploring every nook and cranny of the 25 mile long Lake Taupo and its many feeder streams. That took some doing for there are more than 30 of these entering the lake's 240 square mile expanse. He went to great length to show me the best fishing including forays into the Western Bays, many of which could only be reached by boat.

I was actually there at the wrong season for the best river fishing which occurs in April and May when the larger lake fish swarm up the rivers on their spawning runs, and again in November and December when they are dropping back down to the lake. There were always good resident fish in the river pools and we took a few two to five pound trout in the lower reaches of the Tongariro and in the Waitahanui, Himemaia and Waiotaka rivers along the eastern shore. (Practically all place names in New Zealand are Maori in origin.)

These river rainbows are extremely strong and feisty and often take to the air repeatedly when hooked. The main problem is the clarity of the water, which calls for fine terminal tackle, but if too fine a tippet is used you'll lose the fish you do hook. We usually settled for 1X leader strength, ordinarily considered fairly heavy. Streamer type flies are generally used but I had my best luck drifting a Gold Ribbed Hare's Ear nymph just under the surface.

We also trolled with our fly rods and size 8, 3X long Parson's Glory streamers in the lake itself where I took my largest rainbow of the trip, a silvery 10 pound torpedo.

The entire region around Rotorua and Taupo is volcanic in origin and there is a great deal of thermal activity in the form of geysers, hot springs, steam vents, mud boils, etc. I still have a piece of pumice I found floating in one of the lake's bays. At Taupo they have harnessed the subsurface thermal energy with a large power plant to furnish heating, much as they do in Iceland.

The resident fishermen all agree that overfishing in the past few decades has lessened the average size of the area's rainbows since Zane Grey's day, but there are still a lot of excellent fish to be had.

Wally Jensen and Bob Sullivan had given me a great introduction to their country's fishing, yet even better times were ahead. It began the day I took off to the south, arriving in Wellington in time to catch the 8:00 p.m. car ferry to Lyttleton, which is the port for Christchurch, the South Island's largest city. After a 10 hour overnight crossing I drove off the *Maori Queen* and headed leisurely down along the Pacific coastline.

During my travels in New Zealand, when I wasn't staying with new-found friends, I overnighted at bed-and-breakfast homes. They were quite numerous and at that time were $3.00 per night.

The further south I traveled the more beautiful the country became. Below Dunedin the highway turns west toward Queenstown and Te Anau. I took the latter route, ending up in that small, picturesque settlement on the eastern shore of Lake Te Anau. Ignoring the large hostelry there I looked around until I found a bed-and-breakfast home, making it my headquarters for the next several days. During this time I fished in the Waiau River between lakes Te Anau and Manapouri and in the Mararoa River that flows into the Waiau.

While New Zealand's North Island is famous for the large rainbows of its lake systems, and is best fished with the wet fly or streamer, the South Island waters fish better with the dry fly and floating line. They also offer a greater variety of quiet, secluded surroundings. Brown trout predominate on the South Island but there are also rainbows and landlocked salmon in many of its waters.

In the Waiau near Manapouri I fished from shore, the water being too deep to wade, over visible legions of huge brown trout, lined up like the hordes of Attila the Hun. I must admit my success ratio there was low, consisting of a couple of three pound fish taken on a weighted nymph. There were dozens I could see of three times that size. I later found out that these trout were heavily angled for by the local threadliners (spin fishermen) and as a result were extremely wary. Elsewhere I had better luck, particularly when I drove the 80 mile mountain track to Milford Sound.

This area is the wildest part of New Zealand. There are no towns and few inhabitants along the route which traverses the heavily forested range on a narrow, gravel-surfaced road. Heading northwest from Te Anau the road goes up the Eglinton River valley, paralleling the river for miles. I caught and released several nice brown trout along the Knobb's Flat meadows of the medium sized Eglinton and lost one monster of approximately 10 pounds when the hook pulled out. The Kakahi Queen and Blue Dun were the successful dry fly patterns.

I stopped for lunch at a small outpost near Cascade Creek then continued on to the top of the range and through the Homer Tunnel before beginning the long, winding descent to Milford Sound. The last few miles of the track followed the Cleddau River, a large, fast-flowing and boulder-strewn obstacle course that empties into the head of the Sound by the small village of Milford.

Since it was just mid afternoon when I checked into the Milford Hotel I took a two and a half hour launch ride down the 11 mile course of the Sound, past mile high Mitre Peak and three to four thousand foot overhanging cliffs of bare rock, laced with filmy waterfalls, to its entrance into the Tasman Sea.

After a bath, I went into the hotel's lounge and bar for a mug of ale. There I met three young fellows in their late twenties who, as it turned out, were the captain and crew of one of the dozen lobster fishing boats headquartered in the harbor. Before the evening was over they had invited me to spend some time at sea with them. The following three days I lived on board their 46 foot steel-hulled vessel, the *Tradewind*, cruising the uninhabited coast of the Tasman Sea, one of the wildest and most scenic shorelines in the world.

At intervals we lifted the wire cage lobster traps, whose positions were marked with large orange floats, removing their contents, rebaiting with dead fish and lowering them again five or six fathoms to the sea bed. These lobsters are of the Florida variety; that is, they do not have large front claws. The Kiwis call them crayfish. The market price at that time was $2.60 a pound and every trap we lifted had two dozen or more legal lobsters in its meshes. George West and his crew were well on the way to becoming financially secure.

Between experiencing the grandeur of the rugged coastline with its rocky headlands, red stags pacing the beaches and pods of seals in the surf, marveling at the seamanship of the crew as we threaded through countless small islands and reefs and stuffing myself several times a day on fresh lobster and ale, it was a time to be both savored and remembered forever.

Before leaving Milford I fished the Cleddau River a couple of

An intriguing glimpse of falling water off the Milford Sound Track.

times, with only mediocre results, although it is noted for producing some large sea-run browns. On the way back out over the range I took a side track some nine miles to the Hollyford River, a lovely, boulder-studded stream of medium size. I had no luck there but on the drive back out I spotted an intriguing glimpse of falling water off in a side cleft, to the east of Lyttle's Flat. I parked and hiked in through the trackless forest, through groves of beech, Kanuka and 50 foot tall Ponga tree ferns, guided by the sound of falling water.

Fishing this narrow but deep and fast-flowing headwater of

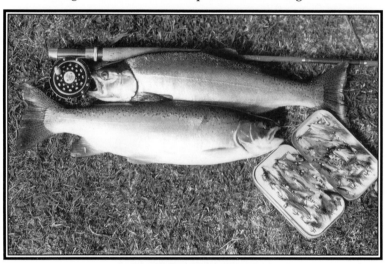

South Island rainbows.

the Hollyford proved to be the single most memorable fishing experience of the entire trip. In the space of an hour, and in the wildest possible setting, casting with a size 14 Twilight Beauty I hooked, fought and landed two streamlined rainbows of six pounds apiece and was thwarted on four more of about the same size. Overhanging limbs of the Kanuka trees and over-eagerness on my part were the contributing factors. A couple were lost due to striking too quickly, resulting in less than a solid hook-up . . . the consequence of seeing the fish coming to the fly through the crystalline water.

Surrounded by exotic vegetation, with rugged peaks towering above and complete silence except for the music of running water and the occasional mellifluous call of a bell-bird, it was a time of complete and exciting isolation from the modern world.

I did a considerable amount of fairly successful fishing and enjoyable sightseeing on the way back north, particularly around lakes Wanaka, Hawea, Wakatipa and their feeder streams, but the fishing along the Milford Track was the highlight of my time spent in that friendly country below the Southern Cross.

Addenda:

Although New Zealand angling certainly is very productive by North American standards, because of its popularity with fishermen from other countries and the ease of access to most of its waters, the Eldorado days of 40 years ago have gone and today it takes more seeking and stalking to take the better fish.

There is a lot of threadlining but on the whole New Zealand is predominantly a fly fishing environment. I'd estimate that overall its trout, both browns and rainbows, average two to three pounds but run to five or six pounds in some areas and in a few to 10 pounds or more.

Private water seldom exists in New Zealand. Landowners are not permitted to charge for rights of entry for angling, providing of course that permission is sought. If you are properly licensed you can fish just about anywhere.

I'd be inclined to recommend April and May (equivalent to our autumn) for both islands, with November and December a second choice. It is only 15 hours away by air, its people are extremely friendly and helpful and its scenic delights alone make a visit well worthwhile.

Chapter 18
Magellanic Magic

Three years after my first venture there, I was back in Patagonia. It was absolutely necessary to my mental health that I return. I had barely tapped its superlative angling variety on the first trip and had since spent many nights dreaming of its solitude, its grandeur and its relatively unexplored waters—more than any man could fish in his lifetime.

From Brownsville, Texas it was a 12 hour flight to Santiago, Chile, including short stops at Panama City and Lima, Peru. The following day I arrived in Puerto Montt via Lan Chile Airlines. This Pacific fishing port is the take-off point for the Straits of Magellan and beyond. I made arrangements to take passage on a small Servicio Maritimo steamer and spent the next six days in a cruise down the rugged Chilean coastline, perhaps the wildest region on the globe other than the Arctic and the Antarctic deserts.

The coastal landscape is dominated by the towering Andes. They form the backbone of the South American continent, stretching in almost unbroken array from the Caribbean Sea through the Patagonian ice cap. The greatest peaks are second only to the Himalayas in height. More than 20 summits are over 15,000 feet above sea level and no less than a dozen are well over 20,000 feet. Aconcagua, the Chilean giant at 22,829 feet, is the highest mountain in the Western Hemisphere. Many of the peaks are volcanic, showing dormant life in the plumes of smoke windblown from their cones.

Below these crests is some of the world's finest scenery with many glaciers and snow-filled cirques. Silver strands of streams are set in a matrix of velvet green forests, dotted with scores of lovely, lonely lakes.

Several hundred miles of the fjord-indented coastline between Puerto Montt and Cape Froward reveal the roughest and largest uninhabited region imaginable. Offshore are thousands of islands. Navigation through these often storm tossed waters is a full-time chore.

We finally arrived at Punta Arenas (Sandy Point), a town of about 20,000 population overlooking the northern shore of the Straits of Magellan. At 53 degrees south latitude, it is the southernmost city in the world. There is only one permanent settlement further south; Ushuaia, on the Argentine side of Tierra del Fuego.

My journey there was the backdrop for a whole series of unusual angling adventures that could comprise an entire volume in themselves, beginning with taking brown trout directly out of the Straits of Magellan at the mouth of the Rio Agua Fresca and including side bus trips to reach such fabled waters as the Rio Gallegos, Rio Ciainke, Rio Serrano, Rio Grey, Rio San Jose and the Rio Penitente.

All of these waters were packed with trout. For sheer numbers I'd give the Penitente first place but for sizable fish the Gallegos and Serrano were notable holding many browns in the eight to 10 pound range. Of them all I enjoyed fishing the Rio Serrano the most, largely because of the fantastic terrain it flows through. It is a fairly short but broad river, about the width of Wyoming's Madison River, and runs from Lago Toro southwest into the glaciated Last Hope Sound.

The region is dominated by an unbelievable grouping of huge granite peaks known as the Torres del Paine (Towers of Piney). It is difficult, if not impossible, to adequately describe the wild magnificence of these peaks. I was born and raised in mountain country and love all high places but I have never seen anything to compare with the Paine for sheer massiveness and savage beauty. They make the Grand Tetons look like mere foothills.

This southernmost 300 miles of the continent is among the windiest regions in the world. The wind blows without let-up 24 hours a day, for weeks on end. No gentle zephyrs—the velocity ranges from 30 to 40 mph, with gusts up to 70 mph. You need a fairly stiff fly rod of 8 1/2 or 9 feet that can handle a 9 or 10 weight-forward line and you often have to pick wading spots on the windward side of the river where cut banks or tree groves somewhat nullify the gale. There are periods when, regardless of how clever your double-haul casting, you cannot adequately cover the water. The wind is often accompanied by driving rain squalls which can last from a few minutes to all day. Such conditions do make fishing difficult but the numbers, the size and the eagerness of the fish are certainly worthwhile rewards for the discomfort involved.

Fly patterns that had the most success within this area were the Muddler Minnow and large streamers of the Platinum Blonde and Honey Blonde designs, tied on size 6-3X hooks.

Following a week or two of fishing these waters I embarked on an adventurous trip that had been my primary reason for being there. In Punta Arenas I made arrangements with a local pilot, Antonio Rubio, for a flight into the upper Rio Grande in Tierra del Fuego.

I met Antonio at the local airfield one morning at 9:00 a.m. We were soon airborne in his Beechcraft Cherokee. Flying over the

A sea-run brown from the Rio Grande.

40 mile expanse of the Straits and into the interior of Tierra del Fuego was a trip of about an hour and 30 minutes. Fuego is extremely wild, rolling and mainly treeless country. There are a few isolated sheep estancias which from the air appear as mere fly-specks on its surface.

Antonio set the plane down on an emergency landing strip after first buzzing it to chase off a herd of wild guanacos. From there it was just a quarter of a mile to the river where a streamside grove of gnarled dwarf coihue trees afforded a windbreak for my small tent and sleeping bag. A fresh water spring and plenty of dry, dead limbs for firewood were handy.

After helping me get the tent set up Antonio returned to his plane, promising to come back for me in seven days.

The weather was overcast but not too windy so I wasted no time in rigging up and getting into the river. The Rio Grande averages about 80 yards in width and the bottom is mainly gravel. It has a good current but no broken or really fast water, and I could wade across it in many places. Its serpentine course winds across the rolling prairie landscape from its source in Lago Blanco a hundred kilometers to the Atlantic Ocean. Here and there along its course are copses of wind-deformed trees but for the most part the landscape is open and covered with short grasses and shrubs.

Birds are everywhere: Andean and ashy-headed geese by the thousands, many species of ducks, small owls, swifts, falcons and kites. Nomadic bands of the flightless rheas were often seen from a distance. I tried on several occasions to stalk within photo range but they proved to be as wary as the guanacos. I never did get within less than 100 yards of them.

As for the fishing it left little to be desired. Every run and bend had its quota of trout; mainly browns but occasional rainbows, ranging from pip squeaks of 14 or 15 inches to their elders, measured in pounds. I was disappointed never to tangle with one of the huge 15 to 18 pound sea-run browns. They were late in running that year. River residents of five and six pounds certainly furnished enough action to keep even the most blasè angler contented.

One interesting discovery I quickly made was that these fish feed largely on a small fresh water snail. Nearly every fish I landed had its stomach so full of these snails that its belly felt like a bean bag. Despite this they came to the large streamers I used quite readily. I kept only an occasional small one for the pot. Their flesh, probably as a result of the crustacean diet, was bright red and of excellent flavor.

Of the week I was there, two days of wind-driven torrential rain kept me in camp. The rest of the time I ranged up and down the river, packing a lunch of bread, cheese and raisins in the back of my fishing vest and taking shelter wherever I could find it during intermittent rain squalls. There was frost at night but the days were not too cold, ranging in the high 50s and low 60s. I actually experienced two enjoyable rare days of no wind at all. On such occasions the utter stillness, except for an isolated bird or animal call, and the vast open reaches of space with no other humans about, lent an almost unearthly air to my wanderings.

All too soon the week passed and Antonio returned, right on time, to pick me up. It was a clear day and our return flight across the Bahia Inutil and Laguna de Los Cisnes, then over the Straits of Magellan to Punta Arenas, offered many grand views of this stern but enchanting country.

That afternoon I arranged a flight to Puerto Montt and took off the following morning for a full day's passage over hundreds of miles of the great glacier-strewn Andes cordillera, arriving late in the evening, tired but with an additional store of many more pools of memory.

Chapter 19

POOLS OF MEMORY

Dream Stream

Prior to venturing into the Magellanic realm of the winds I had contacted Raul San Martin and made arrangements to meet him in Esquel on March 2. It was now February 27, 1970 and I was faced with the problem of getting from Puerto Montt on the Chilean coast across the Andes into Argentina.

I had previously read about a route between the two countries that was considered by many travelers to be the most beautiful single mountain passage in the world. I had to experience that. A short walk from my hosteria to the Turisur Office enabled me to secure a ticket for the trip, to begin at 7:30 the following morning.

I retired early and rose at dawn to the beginning of a bright, clear day. The ensuing trip was so complicated and so full of scenic wonders that I must rely on my field notes to recall the details.

From Puerto Montt, the mecro (bus) journeyed through rolling foothills to the village of Puerto Varas on Lago Llanquihue, then east to Petrohue. Following the Rio Petrohue upstream we arrived at its outlet from Lago Todos Los Santos near the base of Mount Osorno, one of Chile's most impressive volcanic peaks. Osorno's symmetry, rising from a nearly circular base 50 miles in diameter to a snow-capped cone 9,000 feet above, closely resembles Japan's Mt. Fujiyama.

I knew the Petrohue Canyon's green currents were the habitat of some great trout but I had no time to dally there.

We boarded the small steamer, *Esmeralda,* and threaded through the islands of Lago Todos Los Santos to Puella at its eastern end. This is the body of water that Teddy Roosevelt called, "The most beautiful lake in the world."

After a fine lunch at the hosteria in Puella we journeyed over the Perez Rosales Pass by bus. We were now in the heart of the Andes, on a narrow, one-lane unsurfaced road. There is an interesting system worked out there in which travel goes only one way in the mornings and in the opposite direction in the afternoons. Our route was largely through heavy forests of linga, coihue and pines with openings here and there offering glimpses of spectacular glaciated peaks such as the volcanic El Tronador (The Thunderer).

90

A short stop at Casa Panque to check through the Chilean border patrol post preceded a drive down to Puerto Frias and the Argentine border post.

Boarding another boat, we toured the length of Laguna Frias to Puerto Alegre then switched to a bus for Puerto Blest, which is on the western arm of the sprawling Lago Nahuel Huapi. There we took yet another boat ride of three hours to Llao Llao. One last change to a mecro took us to our final destination, the city of San Carlos de Bariloche. The boat and bus exchanges all went off smoothly and when it was over I had to agree with the statement I had read concerning the journey's superior reputation.

The first available bus from Bariloche to Esquel didn't leave until Monday morning so I secured a room in a private residencia and spent the weekend in and around the picturesque city, eating, exchanging escudos for pesos and sightseeing. The highlight of the weekend occurred on Saturday afternoon when I took a taxi drive up the northern shore of Lago Nahuel Huapi to Boca Totorel on the Brazo Bonito arm and, in an hour's fishing (while the cab driver took a siesta), landed and released two brook trout in the four to five pound range.

The Esquel bus left at 7:00 a.m., the all-day trip again being through the mountains, skirting many lovely lakes and dozens of cascading streams all of which the driver assured me held Arco iris or Truchas de arroyos. At that point I fervently daydreamed of four straight months of expense-free time wherein I could fish every one of them.

Reaching Esquel, I was really happy to meet with Raul again. This young Argentinean had proved to be a knowledgeable guide and a great camping and fishing companion. Short (about 5'5") and dark haired, he has a ready smile that stays in place through any difficulties encountered. He is a skilled mechanic with both boat and automobile engines, which is a necessity in that country where garage facilities may be hundreds of kilometers apart. He knows the backcountry well and is a perceptive and enthusiastic angler. What more could one ask of a pilgrimage partner?

Raul informed me that the border dispute between Chile and Argentina had flared up again and one could not get past the Chilean outpost on Lago General Paz. He said he knew of more lake systems with plenty of big brook trout and one river he wanted to show me. By now I don't believe I have to confirm the fact that I'm a brook trout fanatic. I'd rather catch one sizable square-tail than a dozen big rainbows or browns.

So once again we ventured out on the horrific Patagonian roads in Raul's battered Jeep station wagon, heading south between the foothills and the pampas. Passing the turnoff to Lago Paz, we kept on through the village of Gobanador Costa to the Rio Senguerr which is the outlet of our destination, Lago Fontana. A side track followed the river west to the lake, where we set up our tent camp on the shoreline.

Fontana is a wide-spread lake with many forested islands. At its western end it is joined to another, smaller lake, Lago La Plata, by a short stretch of river. Both lakes are in Argentina, the border following the crest of the cordillera that rings the western side of La Plata. Most of our fishing was done by wading the connecting river and at the mouths of smaller streams entering the dark blue-green depths of Lago Fontana. The trout there are mainly brookies with an occasional rainbow in the faster inlet currents. We caught many more fish here than we had at Lago General Paz and did not see or take a trout of less than four pounds. In one evening Raul and I caught and released 40 brook trout from four to eight pounds! It sounds incredible but it is not an exaggeration. For productivity of big squaretails these Patagonian lakes are far ahead of any North American waters.

After four days of this angler's nirvana we packed up and returned over the tortuous trail to Esquel. Following a day's rest, we launched Raul's boat in Lago Futalaufquen and cruised to its

Dream stream—the Rio Rivadavia.

head, where we entered the Arrayanes River. The Arrayanes flows out of Lago Verde, which in turn is fed by the Rio Rivadavia, coming from its source in Lago Rivadavia. These connecting waterways are full of trout but one stretch, the Rio Rivadavia, was outstanding.

Each fisherman, I suppose, has his own idea of angling paradise, varying with personal make-up and preferences. For me, a fishing paradise needs to be moving water, in the mountains and in a forested area, although the stream itself can be flowing

92

through meadow openings. It should be of medium size so that both banks can be covered by casting from midstream. The bottom should be of easily wadeable gravel and sand, with boulder-strewn pocket water here and there. The presence of wildlife along the banks and the songs of various forest birds complete the scenario.

Such a stream is the Rio Rivadavia. It is the only river I know of that is superior in beauty of water and surroundings to anything I've experienced in our own Rocky Mountain waters. In width, it is about the size of the Gallatin River. Its banks are lined with thickets of lacy bamboo and groves of arrayan (myrtle) and coihue, with calls of tintica, chucao, bandurria and other exotic bird life.

The Rio Rivadavia flows like molten glass, cold as glacier melt. The light turquoise tint of its currents does not cloud its transparency. You can see every pebble on the bottom in 15 to 20 feet of water where the pools are deep and smooth surfaced. Its brook trout are among the most colorful of their kind. It is amazing that, given the extreme clarity of the water, you can never spot

A male brookie in spawning regalia is the most handsome of fresh water fishes.

one until it is twisting on your line. These fish are a superb example of nature's protective patterning.

Beginning at the outlet of Lago Rivadavia, Raul and I spent several hours drifting down the enchanting river, beaching the boat at intervals so we could wade its sparkling runs. We had almost constant action from one to three pound brookies, with an occasional rainbow coming to the fly. I recall Raul's shouts of simulated annoyance while trying to subdue a seven pound rainbow that was taking up his valued brook trout battling time. These squaretails were not big fish for that country but would be an angler's prize anywhere else.

I was using a dry hairwing stonefly pattern while Raul fished a weighted March Brown nymph. There was little to choose between the success of both. It was a wonderful day. From a lifetime of fishing adventures, the Rio Rivadavia will always be remembered as my personal dream stream.

Once back in Esquel it was with great reluctance that I said farewell to Raul, one of the finest young men I was ever to meet in my travels.

Addenda:

It is an interesting fact that there were no fresh water game fish in Argentina and Chile until just after the turn of this century. In 1903-04 hatcheries were established at Rio Blanco in Chile and at San Carlos de Bariloche in Argentina. Eggs and fry of brown trout were introduced from England, those of brook trout and land locked salmon from Maine and rainbows from California. This stocking was an ecologist's dream. No predator fish existed and the primordial waters were full of small forage fish, crustaceans and aquatic insect life. The resulting hatchery stocks were widely scattered throughout Patagonia, largely by air drops, and the rest is angling history.

Despite other claims, Patagonia is the only place in the world I know of where you can still experience fishing as it was in the beginning. Wherever you go, and whatever species of trout you prefer, your chances of hooking many fish and large fish are greater than anywhere else. Despite its growing popularity and traveling opportunities in the last decade or so, plus a few "improvements" of hydroelectric projects, its area is so vast and as yet so unsettled that, even now, there are hundreds of miles of streams and who knows how many lakes that have not yet been touched by the angler's fly. It is the last great frontier of wilderness angling and perhaps the finest our planet will ever know.

Chapter 20

POOLS OF MEMORY

The Big Laxa

Angling for Atlantic salmon *(Salmo salar)* has long been considered the ultimate in fresh water fishing. At the same time it takes an avid and patient fly caster to view them in this light, for they can be the most fickle of fishes and their pursuit monotonous and often frustrating. In most salmon rivers the angler is fortunate to hook a brace of salmon in a full day of fishing. To the *salar* aficionado, however, these are minor considerations well worth enduring for those fantastic periods when the salmon are responding. It is generally agreed that, pound for pound, among fresh water game fish only the fresh-run Pacific steelhead can approach the Atlantic salmon in fighting ability.

I had experienced salmon fishing in the eastern Canadian provinces of Newfoundland, Quebec and Labrador but in the time spent there had not taken any fish over 10 pounds. In talking with Lee and Joan Wulff, whom I had been helping to teach summer fly fishing seminars on Colorado's Elk River, I became really fired up

Lee and Joan Wulff.

with the idea of taking a good sized salmon and of doing so in what Lee declared were nearly ideal conditions. Following their advice I contacted Fish & Game Frontiers, Inc., an international travel consultant, and made reservations for a trip to Iceland the following year (1974).

Iceland has been called the land of frost and fire. It lies just below the Arctic Circle, about midway between New York and Moscow. The entire island area of 39,768 square miles was created by volcanoes and today earth's inner fires still burn not far under its surface. There is no need for furnaces in Iceland. The buildings are heated with natural hot water piped in from extensive thermal areas. Eighty percent of the land is uninhabited, with approximately half the population of 205,000 living in the capitol city of Reykjavik.

The climate is mild along the coast, influenced by a northern extension of the Gulf Stream. Reykjavik has milder winters than New York or Chicago. Deep fjords indent the coastline and mountains, many bearing year-round glaciers and ranging to 9,000 feet in elevation lie inland.

Iceland has some 60 rivers, practically all of which support salmon runs. Their fish have not been pillaged at sea and they have managed their rivers well, using angling as the major harvesting method. All the rivers are under private ownership and control. The sport they afford today reflects one of the most progressive fisheries managements in the world.

Salmon begin ascending the rivers early in June and continue to arrive throughout July and August. American travel agencies such as the one I had signed up with make lease arrangements with Icelandic landowners and maintain fishing rights for their clients on some of the best rivers.

During the first week in August I took off from New York on an eight and a half hour overnight flight via Icelandic Airlines, arriving in the international airport at Keflavik by 9:30 a.m. A check through customs was followed by a 40 mile bus ride to Reykjavik and an overnight stay at the Saga Hotel. The following afternoon the last lap of the journey was an hour and a half flight to Husavik on the northeastern coast of the island.

We were met at the crushed lava airstrip by our guides and transported in English LandRovers to the fishing lodge in the valley of the Laxamyri River. The sign in front of the lodge proclaimed this to be the Veidiheimilid Arnesi, or Fishermen's Home on the Arness Farm. This is altogether separate from the main farm buildings and has its own kitchen staff, a sunny dining room, cozy lounge with fireplace, a tackle room with boot dryers, separate sleeping rooms, showers and a sauna, the latter being one of the greatest remedies for aching muscles ever invented.

The Laxamyri, also called the Laxa i Adaldal (Salmon River

in the Adaldal Valley), has been aptly termed by Lee Wulff as the Queen of Icelandic rivers. It is the second largest river in that country and is noted for the large size of its salmon, the average running over 13 pounds. Its source is islanded Lake Myvatn from whence it flows north through a broad pastoral valley, emptying into the sea at Husavik.

The guides or ghillies live in the immediate vicinity. Transportation to the various river beats was by LandRover. The typical fishing day began with an early breakfast then a change into fishing gear and a drive to your assigned beat. There were eight beats or stretches of water extending along seven or eight miles of river. Each angler fishes two different beats in each of the fishing periods which extend from 7:00 a.m. to 1:00 p.m. and from 4:00 p.m. to 10:00 p.m. This works out well as everyone has a chance to try all the available water.

Originally there were seven anglers in our party but one had to leave after the first day. The ghillies were all great—knowledgeable and conscientious. My guide, for example, was Heimar Gudmundson a short, gnome-like character in his 60s who had fished the Big Laxa as he called it for some 40 years and claimed a lifetime score of more than 3,000 salmon. I was a bit concerned about him at first for he carried a jug of Icelandic liquor called Brennivin under his jacket and sipped on it at frequent intervals all day long. My concern proved groundless for Heimar was always in control, though perhaps just a trifle unsteady on rare occasions. One evening when I was feeling stiff and tired, I accepted a swallow from his bottle and quickly realized why it is referred to as "The Black Death."

Although the fishing started slowly it proved to be even more than I had hoped for. The first evening produced no fish for any of our party. The following morning I was assigned to Beats 3 and 4. In the lower stretch of Beat 3 (Skrioufluo) a 15 pound hen fish took my size 6 Cosseboom fly and was netted by Heimar after a great 10 minute struggle. That afternoon I fished Beats 5 and 6 but with no further action and my morning's fish was the only salmon taken that day.

This type of fishing is not a diversion to be taken lightly or a pastime for the unbeliever. Salmon fishing demands determination and staying power—the same qualities possessed by the fish. To be successful the angler must stick with it no matter how discouraging conditions may be. The only major difficulty we encountered, other than initial reluctance of the fish to hit, was a considerable amount of floating moss in the river which required frequent inspection and cleaning of the fly and leader knots.

The second day fishing picked up dramatically and all of the party took fish. In morning from Beats 1 and 2 I caught salmon of six, 12 and 11 pounds and in the evening from Beat 4, another of 15 pounds.

A brace of 20 pound salmon from the Big Laxa.

The following day I had no action in the morning Beats of 5 and 6. There are a few beats on the river that are too deep to wade and so must be fished by boat, the ghillie holding it steady above the best lies while the angler systematically covers the water on both sides and below with lengthening casts. The upper part of Beat 2 (Skerfluoir) is one of the boat pools. Standing in the rear of the small rowboat that afternoon I had not made more than three or four casts when something that looked like a waterlogged chunk of pulpwood detached itself from the bottom and angled up toward the double-hooked Nighthawk. Engulfing the fly it turned and sank from sight, whereupon I struck as hard as I dared. Feeling the hook, the salmon surged up and cleared the river's surface in a tremendous leap. It was a huge, dark male with heavy kype and a caudal fin the size of a dinner plate.

I fought him from the boat for 10 minutes, during which he made several more jumps and took me well into the line backing on long, surging runs.

Finally it looked like I had him coming a bit so Heimar beached the boat and I continued the fight from shore. By that time the moss was building up on the leader, especially just above the hook's attachment to the corner of his jaw. Another five minutes and I nearly had him close enough for Heimar's long-handled net. Then, suddenly, he was gone. The moss had built up to the point where a ball of several pounds of it had given the fish enough leverage to tear free. Both Heimar and I judged that salmon to weigh very close to 30 pounds. I was heartsick. It was

98

one fine battle while it lasted and certainly one of the top experiences in 60 years of angling.

The next three days were action-packed for all hands. My best period occurred one afternoon back on the Skrioufluo. I had fished the main part of the pool without success. Then, just above the tailout ledge I spotted what I was looking for: the porpoise-like head and tail rise that betokens a fish ready to take. Three times I swam the size 8 Blue Doctor by him and each time he rejected it at the last second. On the fourth drift he was on solidly—that unbelievable surge of raw power that takes line flying through the guides.

Four times I worked him out of the mid river currents and four times he hurled himself back into them. Everything held and I finally shouted to Heimar. Arising laboriously from his grassy couch the ghillie tacked to and fro through the greensward tussocks to the river bank, where on the second try he got the net under the salmon and lifted it ashore. A bit over 20 pounds. This was what I had hoped for.

I took a total of four salmon that day and three more the next, while losing two or three others to moss buildup. One of those I landed had both mine and a second fly in the corner of his jaw. Have you ever caught a fish that had another angler's fly imbedded in its mouth? This doesn't happen often, not nearly so often as one might suppose. Fish seem to be able to get rid of a fly easily. I have a good idea how they do this, as on another trip I lay on a rock ledge overlooking a gravel-bottomed pool below the Whale River's lpaluk Falls and watched a salmon I had hooked and lost turning on its side, rubbing its jaw in which the Muddler Minnow fly was lodged against the gravel.

On the last evening's session I lost another tremendous fish in the Graustraumar (Beat 1). We were allowed to fish until noon on the final day. I ended up on Beat 3 again where I lucked out with another 20 pounder taken with the same Blue Doctor fly the big one had nabbed the night before.

It had been a notable week. Our six rods accounted for 76 salmon. Several were 20 pounds or better with the best fish being 24 1/2 pounds. Ours was the best week's take for the 1974 season on the Laxamyri.

I have since made more than one return trip to the Big Laxa, with varying success, but the initial visit remains the strongest in my store of memories.

Addenda:

Over a comparatively short span of years, salmon runs in many of the once-great angling rivers of the world—in the north-eastern United States, Canada and Scandinavia, the British Isles and many in Europe as far south as Spain and Portugal—have either been lost completely or badly decimated by various causes, all man-made. In 1965 the major international feeding ground for salmon was discovered in the Davis Straits off the southwest coast of Greenland. After many subsequent years of drift netting these fish the activity was finally reduced but not until severe damage to the stocks had occurred.

Other factors have contributed to the salmon's decline. In a world where man has polluted, poisoned, dammed, channeled, diverted and silted most of the once-great rivers the crystalline streams of Iceland afford one of the last great unspoiled retreats for the salmon angler. It is expensive, but not out of reach, and is a quest the avid trout fisherman should be able to delight in at least once in his lifetime. The power and spectacular fighting ability of *Salmo salar* has to be experienced to be fully appreciated.

Chapter 21

Killey Water

My mother's side of the family were all Scots: Stirlings, Maitlands and MacKenzies. Her family name, MacKenzie, was passed on to me as a middle name.

Father's side of the family was of Scottish and German mix. I always figured that made me three quarters Scotch and a quarter German and because of an ingrained love of the bagpipes, the tartan and all things Scottish, I've always tended to downplay that last quarter.

Extensive research pertaining to the history of Scotland and her Highland clans had imbued me with the desire to see it for myself. In the words of an old Canadian-Scottish boating song: "From the lone shieling of the misty island, mountains divide us, and the waste of seas. Yet still the blood is strong and the heart is Highland, and we in dreams behold the Hebrides."

I knew the various gatherings for Highland Games took place largely in the month of September which was also a good time to sample the trout and salmon fishing. So on a whim, and without much preliminary preparation, I took off late one August from Stapleton Airport in Denver. At Kennedy Airport in New York I transferred and, after an overnight flight, deplaned at Prestwick Field, 30 miles southwest of Glasgow.

After checking through customs I went to pick up my baggage only to find it had not arrived with me. There I was in Scotland with no waders or fishing tackle, to say nothing of a change of clothes.

The lass at the BOAC counter said not to worry; she'd locate the luggage for me. Meanwhile I took a bus into Glasgow and after touring its sights, spent the night at a bed-and-breakfast home.

I called the airport first thing the next morning. The lassie had come through and my baggage had arrived. I took the bus back, collected my gear, signed the rental papers for a little Hillman Hunter sedan and took off to the north.

It was a good thing I'd had previous training in New Zealand with left hand driving for the southern Scottish roads consist mainly of two-way narrow lanes. I hadn't progressed far beyond the Firth of Clyde when a huge truck came barreling around a corner, over the center line, forcing me off the road and up against a moss covered vertical rock cliff. The left wheels were in a ditch and the Hunter was hung up on the axles.

I had hardly digested the situation, however, before three cars stopped, a group of lads emerged, gave a few heave-ho's and "walked" the car back onto the road. A close examination later showed not one scratch as a result of the mishap. The luck of the MacKenzies was at work.

Further north in the Highlands I found the roads were well-surfaced but reduced to one lane, with turn-outs every half mile. There the traffic was very light.

I traveled up twisty mountain roads through increasingly rugged scenery around Loch Lomond and past Lock Awe where, years ago, the world record brown trout of nearly 40 pounds was taken. I stopped at one point to watch two fly fishermen standing in a boat wielding 14 foot rods while their ghillie kept it drifting sideways along the shoreline. They had no luck while I was watching.

Early in the evening I arrived in the colorful west port of Oban. The town was full of people there for the World Piping Championships to be held the next two days. I lucked out again with the very last bed-and-breakfast spot available.

I spent the entire two days at the Piobaireachd competitions, of which there were two. One was the Highland Societies' Gold Medal Championship and the other was an open competition. There were 40 contestants in the first and 30 in the second, including pipers from all over the world: Canada, New Zealand, Australia, United States, etc. I was treated to some very complicated and intricate playing which only a true Scot really appreciates. Some of my friends think the bagpipes sound like cats fighting and much prefer the marches of a military brass band to those of a pipe band. As for me, a brass band leaves me unmoved but I'd follow the call of the pipes into the jaws of hell.

Evenings were spent in a quayside pub getting acquainted with local inhabitants over a few Shandys (dark draft beer with lemon soda) and enormous helpings of fish and chips.

The third day was spent at the Argyllshire Gathering on the outskirts of Oban. Sitting on a grassy hillside beneath overcast but warm skies I thoroughly enjoyed the piping, Highland dancing, caber tossing, the kilted mile and many other athletic events.

The following morning I motored leisurely across the increasingly picturesque countryside through Crianlarich, Tyndrum, Dunedin and up to Braemar. Most of this route wound through the Grampian Mountains, their slopes bare of trees but carpeted with heather, accented here and there with patches of yellow gorse, blue bells and fireweed. At one point I encountered a lone piper standing on a promontory at the head of a wild glen and unobtrusively took a couple photographs of him, silhouetted against the purple sheen of the heather shrouded hills. This scene is preserved on the wall before me.

The land was nearly all open—no fence borders in the mountain reaches. I found I could wander freely just about anywhere and could fish most of the burns I came across without fear of being challenged by irate landowners. I took advantage of this during the drive to Braemar, parking on a turn-out and hiking across the heathered hillsides to reach a tumbling brook where I caught pan-sized brown trout on a size 14 Adams dry fly.

Braemar is a lovely town with many picturesque churches and other very old buildings and with a mountain torrent, the Clunie Water, flowing through its center. In addition to oaks, linden and myrtle trees the hamlet and its watercourse are resplendent with groves of Caledonian pines, hawthorn, hazel and cedars. Flowers are everywhere. Each dwelling has an extensive flower garden, colorful and aromatic with banks of roses, sweet peas, snapdragons, harebells and many more.

Once again I lucked out with the last bed-and-breakfast in town for the next day was the great Braemar Gathering and Highland Games. After obtaining the room I looked up the local Scottish Angling Association headquarters and for a few pence purchased a half-day ticket for access to the Clunie Water. I fished along its wooded course below Braemar to where it empties into the Dee, enjoying the slow wade through and under a canopy of ancient cedars and pines.

As I progressed I experienced a slight nagging on the edge of my mind, a memory of another very similar stretch of stream, but I could not bring it into focus. It was a feeling of being flung backwards many years in time. I tried several times to recall it, then let it slide away as a small wake appeared following the swing of my little Black Ghost streamer. That smallish trout and one more were my only rewards other than just the pure enjoyment of being there. At dusk I walked back up to town and had a couple of Shandys, followed by dinner, after which I strolled among the shops and purchased a handsome pair of trousers in the ancient MacKenzie tartan.

Returning to my lodging, suddenly there it was: the memory was of Granite Creek between the falls and Priest Lake. I silently marveled at how far back it took me and how big and small the world could be at the same time.

Saturday, September 2 dawned bright and clear and stayed so all day. The Gathering was magnificent and the setting grand. A massed group of six pipe bands, led by the MacKenzie Caledonian Band of Dundee, opened the ceremonies by marching into the playing fields in full regalia and with clan banners flying.

It was a bonny mixture of sight and sound only a true Scot could really appreciate. The echoing of the pipes across that glen brought a lump to my throat and tears to my eyes.

The Gathering, with its array of piping, dancing and athletic contests went on all day—a more colorful and exciting spectacle could hardly be imagined. These events, centered on the music and sport of the Highlands, have been taking place for more than a thousand years since the reign of King Malcom Canmore.

I slept soundly that night and soon after daylight started down the valley of the Dee River toward Ballater.

My leisurely journey took me from Bridge End and Ballater down along Dee Side through Dinnet and into Aboyne where I attended yet another Highland Gathering and, in probable imitation of my early forebears, attempted to poach a salmon from the Dee. This is all closed water but there are stretches between hamlets, away from the road and among forest glades, where one can fish a bend or two unobserved. My outlawry went unrewarded, however, resulting in just one hooked salmon that won its freedom on the second leap.

From Aboyne I traveled through Inverness and on to Gairloch on the west coast, then driving over the hills by Shieldag and Badachro to the Kerrydale Farm where I purchased a ticket (70 pence) to fish the Killey Water. This is a lovely stream of 30 to 40 yards in width having many deep pools interspersed with riffles, runs and low falls. Ideal wet fly water. From it I took two fine sea trout of five and six pounds, and near the mouth where it empties into a sea loch, hooked and landed my one and only

On the Killey Water, Scotland.

Scottish salmon, a bright, fresh-run hen fish of about 10 pounds that had somehow escaped the estuary nets, losing much of her silver armoring in the process. All three fish were taken on the same fly, a size 8 hairwing Thunder and Lightning. This was my most memorable day of Highland fishing.

I next drove north through Poolewe and Ullapool to Oykel Bridge hoping to get on the Oykel River but it was solidly closed and patrolled. Later, on the Isle of Skye and its Hebridean neighbors Lewis and Harris, I took advantage of the fact that many of the inns or hostelries have angling rights in nearby lochs and river beats. Any guest who stays overnight is entitled to fish these waters for a very small fee. It is a fine system for the traveling angler. There are Loch Leven (brown) trout in all the small streams and also sea-run trout in the larger ones.

The Hebrides are rugged, stark and quiet. I mentioned to one old-timer I met that it looked as if people would have to make their own entertainment as there didn't appear to be much to do.

"Aye, laddie," he said, "Noothing here but feeshing and fornication and in the winter therrr's noo feeshing!"

In retrospect the thing that impressed me most in my travels through Scotland was the realization that, despite its having been settled long before anyone but the Indians were in North America, large expanses of its Highlands are still wild and open and full of natural life. Of course much of the land, like that in Michigan's Upper Peninsula, is really not suited to agriculture or to industry and thus the population has remained low and fairly stable. The angling can be quite a bit better than I experienced. The summer I was there they'd experienced low rainfall and a majority of the rivers and streams were much lower than normal.

Even so the fishing is but one facet of a Highland journey and one soon discovers that it contains some of the most memorable scenery and people to be found anywhere.

> "Still oe'r these scenes my memory wakes,
> And fondly broods with miser care.
> Time but the impression deeper makes
> As streams their channels deeper wear."
> —Anonymous

Chapter 22

POOLS OF MEMORY

The Sonnicants

Following my overseas ventures, which had strained my financial resources, I settled temporarily in Blackhawk, Colorado commuting daily down 30 mile Clear Creek Canyon and through Golden to Denver where I was employed by the American Sportsman's Club as editor of their *Great Outdoors* magazine. Included in my work was instructing the members in such esoteric subjects as rod building, fly tying and fly fishing techniques.

Denver was, and still is, one of the great hubs for the Rocky Mountain angler. Within a few hours drive are a host of fine fishing areas. During my five years there I managed to reach many of them.

Among my favorite memories of that period is one of a trip into the wilderness of the Wind River Range in Wyoming. This game-rich area between the Great Basin and the buffalo plains had played an important role in early western history. It had long been the homeland of the Eastern Shoshonis and prior to that was inhabited by unknown tribes 20,000 years before any white man set foot in America, as evidenced by numerous pictographs found in the region. These have not been accurately dated nor do present-day Indians know who did them.

The Indian woman, Sacajawea, who with her French Canadian husband guided the Lewis and Clark expedition across the mountains to the Pacific was a Shoshoni. Her final resting place is not far from Fort Washakie.

Trapping in the Wind River region began in 1823 by mountain men employees of the Ashley-Henry Fur Trading Company. Among these wilderness wanderers were such famous frontiersmen as Jedediah Smith, Jim Bridger and William Sublette. Records show that these early fur trappers got along quite well with the Shoshonis, often taking wives from the tribe and at times fighting with the braves against their mutual enemies the Crows, Bannocks and Blackfeet.

Because of the abundance of game and fish in the area various tribes fought for its possession. In 1859 the great Shoshoni Chief, Washakie, faced a final showdown with the invading Crows in the battle of Crowheart Butte. After fierce fighting followed by a stalemate the struggle was concluded by a duel between Big Robber, the Crow Chief and Washakie, which Chief Washakie won, afterwards eating Big Robber's heart in triumph.

On the highway between the present towns of Lander and Dubois is the small Indian village of Crowheart where, within sight of the road to the east, can plainly be seen 6,764 foot Crowheart Butte where the epic battle took place.

The first week-long encampment or rendezvous of mountain men took place at Three Crossings on the Sweetwater River in 1824. Several later spring gatherings between 1830 and 1840 were held near the junctions of Horse Creek and Cottonwood Creek with the Green River. At these later events many friendly Indians such as the Shoshonis, Arapaho, Flatheads and Nez Perces also took part in the ceremonies and trading.

The entire present Primitive Area of the Wind River Range is Shoshoni-Arapaho reservation land. Within the range there are no roads, only horse and foot trails. No hunting is allowed except by the Indians and wildlife such as elk, antelope, mule and whitetail deer, black bear and the largest band of bighorn sheep south of the Canadian border are still numerous. The hundreds of mountain lakes and uncounted miles of streams within the region are home to native cutthroat trout plus introduced Eastern brook trout, rainbows, and in a few of the larger lakes, Mackinaws. Anyone can fish the waters of the Wind River Range by purchasing a special permit from the Shoshoni Tribal Council.

Having determined to spend a vacation period in this storied land I drove to Fort Washakie, purchased my angling permit and, upon inquiring about a guide, was referred to Bud LeClair. A visit to his nearby ranch proved very interesting. His home held a wonderful collection of early western weapons, costumes and gear. Bud was the direct descendent of one of the early fur traders in the Fort Bridger area. He gave me directions to his horse camp in the St. Lawrence Basin to the north, and said one of his young Indian wranglers would be happy to serve as my guide.

After some 18 miles of extremely rough and rocky road I made it to the 8,000 foot horse camp on St. Lawrence Creek that evening. I introduced myself to Tom Boyd and his friend, Wayne Archambault, who lived with their wives in a large house trailer. Tom (Bud LeClair's grandson) is a full-blooded Shoshoni and Wayne is a member of the Assiniboin tribe. They had recently returned from a tour of duty in Vietnam and were happy, to say the least, to be back in this ancestral home.

At 9:00 a.m. the following morning Tom and I took off on horseback with a packhorse carrying our gear and food, traveling for six hours through increasingly beautiful country and enjoying frequent encounters with elk and deer. Our trail wound up through Indigo Basin, across Windy Ridge, along Wilson Creek to

In the high mountain streams of Wyoming the catch is always more than trout.

Raft Lake and the upper valley of the North Fork of the Little Wind River. We went past Twenty Lakes and across Entigo Creek, Wolf Creek and Glacier Creek before climbing to Upper and Lower Sonnicant Lakes at the eastern foot of the Continental Divide. Elevation here was 10,000 feet.

To the west of Upper Sonnicant, Prairie Falcon Peak rises in a series of steep terraces and cliffs to 11,348 feet. From our campsite between the two lakes as well as along the Kagewah Pass trail to the southwest, we often saw bands of magnificent bighorn sheep.

The two Sonnicant lakes are joined by a quarter mile stream, bisected with a 20 foot waterfall. Both lakes and the stream were full of Eastern brook trout.

Our camp was a half-size teepee (10 foot diameter) that Tom had made plus our sleeping bags and open, stone-ringed fire pit. The setting with the upper lake and rugged crags in the background was extremely picturesque. Although I had my ever-present 35mm camera along I have, to my regret, no photographs of the trip. Just before setting out I had put a fresh roll of film in the camera but the take-up spool did not engage the film, so although the film-advance lever worked normally it did not wind the film. After supposedly taking 36 pictures I found I had nothing but an unused roll of film.

I thought I had taken the ride in well until I climbed off my mare, Bawly. My bad hip was so stiff I could barely stand but a good night's rest, together with the prospect of the next day, did wonders to ease it. By sun-up I had recovered enough to take a couple of 14 inch brookies from the upper lake for our breakfast. Although it was the latter part of July there were still 10 foot banks of snow around our campsite which served handily to store fish and other foodstuffs until used.

Tom said the country had not been trapped since the early 1940s. There were several pine marten in the area and, evidently unused to man's incursions, they carried out raiding forays in our camp during the night. We purposely left uneaten portions of fish and other food out for them, providing them with a handout and ourselves with an efficient disposal system.

Tom proved to be a great camp companion. Not too talkative he was always pleasant and eager to help. He also loved to fish. One day while we were eating lunch he told me of how the Shoshonis once obtained trout. They would make an improvised dam across a stream, he said, which allowed the water to pass through but stopped all solid matter. Then two or three braves, mounting their ponies, would lash the water with long forked poles while they sang their medicine song and drove the fish upstream toward the dam. The frightened trout, darting forward, would be held against the dam until the Indians waiting there had caught enough to fill their parfleches.

During the ensuing days we traveled, sometimes on foot and sometimes by horseback, to many other waters such as Wykee, Solitude, Heebeecheeche, Polaris and Movo Lakes and to many smaller unnamed ponds and connecting streams. Everywhere we fished we caught trout, the majority being heavily spotted cut-throats. Of them all my favorite spot was the inlet of the stream into Lower Sonnicant Lake. One evening, standing in one spot, I caught and released more than 50 brook trout between 12 and 18 inches. The flies that worked for us were small streamers of the Bloody Butcher and Undertaker patterns with one major exception. Early one evening, just after the wind had died down and the lake surface was calm, I noticed a tremendous rise of fish on Upper Sonnicant. Wading out I discovered the fish were taking advantage of a wayward flight of large black, flying ants. I didn't have an ant imitation with me but a Black Gnat proved to be close enough to fool many of the cruising brookies. The action was fast and furious for an hour or so.

The days passed all too quickly and it was soon time to head back out. The evening before we were to leave I caught and kept a half dozen nice brookies from the Lower Sonnicant inlet burying the dressed-out fish in a snowdrift overnight, with a sprig of spruce to mark the spot. In the morning while Tom was packing our gear I dug out the trout cache, only to find it empty. Our friend the marten had uncovered the cache, made off with the fish and then filled the two foot deep hole with snow! The marker twig was left undisturbed. Small footprints across the drift were the only tangible evidence left by the night raider.

Our leisurely ride back out over the 20 miles of trail was made in about five hours. By the time we reached the horse camp, although a trifle stiff, I felt much better than I had on the trip in.

I plan on getting back there again sometime. The Wind River Range is great country and the Shoshonis have been excellent guardians of its environment. When I do go back I hope I will find it relatively unchanged. At any rate, it's surely worth the time to find out.

Chapter 23

POOLS OF MEMORY

Broadwater

Another of my expeditions, made the same year as the Wind River trip, began from Cooke City, Montana just north of Yellowstone Park. A friend had told me to look up Bill Sommers there as he knew the backcountry well and would make horseback trips for $12.00 per person per day, furnishing everything except fishing tackle, sleeping bag and personal gear. (Ah, the good old days and rates!)

Bill and his wife owned the ATA Auto Court in Cooke City, his guiding being a spare-time operation. Stopping in I introduced myself and asked him if he knew of any good brook trout waters. Bill answered that if I'd settle for four or five pounders he knew where they hung out. That's all I needed to know.

The following morning we started out. There were six of us. Bill, his horse, Ranger, his Boxer dog, Bull, Sally, a pack mule, my great little calico cayuse, Old Paint and me. We drove up the Beartooth Highway over Colter Pass then turned off on a side road which ended in a mountain meadow on the banks of the Broadwater River. Unloading the stock from the horse-trailer was quickly accomplished and, saddling the horses and adjusting Sally's pack, we forded the river and set off on a trail paralleling its north side.

The Broadwater is an exceptionally lovely little river averaging 40 or 50 yards in width. Its dancing, sunspeckled runs over beds of bright sand and fine gravel beckoned me like a Lorelei. Bill said it contained both brookies and Montana grayling and I determined to make a stop there on the way back.

This is an area not well-known except to residents of the region. The Broadwater joins the West Fork and Forge Creek to become the Clark's Fork of the Yellowstone, just before crossing the Montana-Wyoming border.

Our ascending trail led up past Curl Lake and Broadwater Lake then turned north across Sodalite Creek. From this point there was no trail. We traveled by Bill's dead reckoning, up around Middle Mountain and past Cliff Lake, through some rough and broken terrain ending on a grassy bench overlooking a small lake, nameless on the maps, but which Bill had christened

111

"Dream Lake" because of its beautiful surroundings.

The trip had taken five hours. We were now in the heart of the Beartooth Mountains and the Gallatin National Forest. We had good grazing for the stock, a protective grove of winter-twisted spruce for our tent and a lake absolutely brimming with pan-size brook trout. Dream Lake was actually overpopulated, with the result that few of the oldest fish exceeded 10 inches in length. One could catch them on any pattern of fly, wet or dry, as fast as one pleased, day or night. It was like having a large freezer full of instant food on the porch. In 15 minutes of fishing, while Bill was setting up our tent, I landed enough for our supper and breakfast.

A big storm blew up that evening with thunder, lightning and hailstones but we had the camp snugged up and supper eaten by then so its only effect was to lull us off to sleep. By morning it had cleared and we set off to explore.

The outlet of Dream Lake poured over a cliff into a small, narrow lake below. I caught one brook trout there of three pounds, and Bill took a slightly larger one on his spinning rod and a size 6 Colorado brass spinner. We saw other, larger fish but could not tempt them. The lake was full of both red and gray scud and small water beetles. When I cleaned the fish I caught, I found its stomach full of scud.

In the afternoon we hiked up the small inlet stream at the head of this lake, through some rough rock slides, to a second lake somewhat larger than the first. The talus slopes were full of pikas and marmots that drove Bull crazy with their warning (or teasing) squeaks and whistles. He was constantly, and fruitlessly, trying to run them down.

In among the rocks, wildflowers were everywhere. Legions of fat bumblebees busily worked over the tangles of honeysuckle, columbines, Indian paint brush, harebells, mountain daisies and those most exquisite of mountain flowers, the shooting stars.

We spent the rest of the day trying to coax large fish out of the second lake but although we had them follow our lures and flies we were largely unsuccessful in getting them to hit. In the evening we hiked back to camp and cooked up the one large trout I had kept. The two of us were not able to finish its delicious orange meat but Bull polished off everything that we couldn't. This was the only fish I kept from the waters around Dream Lake because we could get all we needed for meals right at camp. As we retired, droves of the smaller trout in Dream Lake were jumping like popcorn on a hot stove.

The next morning after a leisurely breakfast we set out again, going up past the second lake following its inlet stream to the third and biggest of the chain. There we managed to land and release three five pound brook trout, one taking Bill's Colorado spinner and the others succumbing to my weighted Hare's Ear nymph. Continuing on up the slopes we reached the fourth and smallest of the lakes. This was entirely above timberline and surrounded with snowdrifts.

Like Dream Lake it offered countless small brookies. In subsequent ventures we came to call the first lake Two Pound Lake, the second, Four Pound Lake and the third, Five Pound Lake because generally these were the size of the trout we took from them.

These alpine lakes seem to have either an abundance of stunted fish or an unknown (but thought to be small) number of large two to five pound trout. Stocking in this region was mostly accomplished by air drops and in many cases, especially in the smaller lakes, it was overdone. Bill had studied the situation and it was his belief that after an initial stocking of a lake the trout grew quite large. At those elevations he said they do not mature enough to spawn until their fourth year. Life span is six or seven years after which the big fish die off. Their offspring then take over the lake and a second phase begins. As brookies were no longer being stocked in that area once the initial cycle was over and the big fish gone, no more that size would appear although the second generation fish in the most food-rich waters can get to be one to two pounds. Therefore the spots holding trophy size fish are steadily diminishing.

I tend to agree with Bill's theory, at least in part, for I have known of other cases of overstocking. If a small number of trout

Bill Sommers and Bull admire a Beartooth brookie.

are introduced to suitable water they tend to increase in both size and numbers at a fast rate. Trout in new, fertile waters have been known to grow at the rate of a pound a year. After several years the average size of the fish is apt to decline, as numbers and competition for food increase. I must add that this theory is pure speculation and I've not been back to the Beartooths to follow up on it. I do know that it is a lot easier to lightly stock a body of water initially than it is to remove an excess of stunted fish later.

In the days that followed we often ventured even farther afield, sometimes using the horses and sometimes not, reaching other waters in the general area such as Upper and Lower Aero Lakes, Moccasin Lake, Cliff Lake and Rough Lake. We also fished Sky Top Creek, above where it flows into the Broadwater, taking small brookies and grayling on Mosquito and Black Gnat dry flies.

On the trip out we took a two hour recess below Broadwater Lake so I could wade the river. That was one of the most enjoyable periods I've ever had astream. It was a warm, sun-speckled afternoon. The brookies and grayling were not large but came eagerly to a drifting fly. The stream bottom was as smooth as a Persian carpet and the water seldom more than thigh deep. The air was full of butterflies and bird song. In a word, idyllic.

I remember one fish and one spot in particular. A beautiful brook trout in a perfect lie—30 feet across from me at a 45 degree upstream angle and a foot out from the bank, in 10 to 12 inches of water and rising steadily to small tan colored mayflies.

I *knew* somehow, just *knew*, that I'd hook that trout with one cast and I did. A simple, uncomplicated side-arm delivery that set the size 16 Ginger Quill down gently some three feet above the plainly visible fish. As the fly drifted down his feeding lane without hesitation he sucked it in and after a short midstream struggle was beached on a gravel bar. The 13 inch brookie was gently released, although at the time I was saving a few fish to eat.

In thinking back I've always recalled that one small instance, among many more major battles, as the ideal angling sequence. From my store of memories, Bill Sommers is remembered as a fine guide and the Broadwater as one of the most beautiful of all our Rocky Mountain streams.

Chapter 24

POOLS OF MEMORY

Bright Angel

I crawled out of my sleeping bag soon after dawn, feeling rested and peaceful. A heavy mist obscured the canyon landscape which I felt was in my favor as it would shield the sun's glare from the water for an hour at least. Other than the stream's murmur and the ratcheting cry of a kingfisher there were no discernible sounds.

Finishing a quick breakfast of bacon and eggs I drowned the remains of my campfire, strung up my little pack rod and descended from the sandy bench under the cottonwoods to the stream's margin. In the time it took to tie a fly to my tippet the light breeze died and an almost oppressive calm settled over the fog-shrouded surroundings. Because of the restricted view it was really difficult to realize that the bubbly, bouldered, clear run at my feet was not really what it appeared to be—a typical high mountain torrent. True there were mountainous formations here but the entire setting was more than a mile below what is considered the earth's normal surface.

I had arrived here late the previous afternoon following a nine mile trip by mule train from the South Rim of the Grand Canyon, over the Bright Angel Trail.

There are somewhere between one and two million visitors annually to the Grand Canyon's north and south rims. Of this number, however, comparatively few ever penetrate its depths and fewer still get to the very bottom by one of the three major foot and mule routes—too much "work" or "discomfort" or "inconvenience" for the average tourist. Probably three quarters of the Park's visitors settle for a short walk to one or two of the stonewalled rim edge viewpoints, take a few snapshots, then take off for the next in their vacation itinerary of "must-see" sights.

Descending the canyon from its rim is a trip down the ladder of time, rung by rung, with each rung representing centuries rather than years. The entire geologic evolution of the earth, over the millions of years since PreCambrian days, are exposed in the various stratas of rock and earth. As you progress you find yourself looking down at the tops of sizable mountains, past which you gradually descend. It is impossible to realize the full scope of distances involved here unless one actually traverses the miles involved.

115

Author testing Bright Angel's canyon pools.

After a lunch and saddle break at Indian Garden Campground, about halfway down, we continued at the plodding but steady pace of the surefooted mules, down through incredible mixes of formations and colors, to the canyon's bottom. The half dozen other riders continued in to Phantom Ranch, a small layout on Bright Angel Creek that provided rooms and meals for a limited number of visitors. I chose to stay at the Cottonwood Camp some distance upstream from the ranch and was fortunate in having typically dry and mostly sunny weather during the three days I spent there.

Bright Angel Creek was given its name by the explorer, John Wesley Powell, during his epic exploration of the Colorado River in the late 1860s. I understand he gave it that name because of its bright contrast with several silty and discolored feeder streams previously encountered. I thought it was indeed a mountain brook that had somehow become lost and ended up in a most unlikely setting.

As I knelt beside a long, rippled, gravel-bordered run I noticed that the mist was burning off much faster than I had anticipated. I also began to see activity over the stream: cliff swallows skimming low across the water, giving advance notice of an oncoming hatch.

Another few minutes and a surface boil 30 feet away accompanied the slurp of a good fish. Then another, farther down the run. Heavy trout in the subsurface currents were intercepting emerging caddis nymphs. I had originally tied a small size 10 Silver Doctor streamer, a good searching fly, to the leader which I now quickly exchanged for a size 14 weighted Gold Ribbed Hare's Ear nymph. I sent it out across the bubbly current some 10 feet above the first rise noted. It quickly sank below the surface film and, although I couldn't see it, I felt it pause in its drift. Something struck and struck hard. As my rod came up in response, whatever it was took complete control and rocketed upstream. Everything held and eventually I slid an exhausted 22 inch rainbow into the shallows where I unhooked and held him upright in the current until he regained strength enough to wriggle out of my grasp. This was not only the first but, save one other of an inch longer, was the largest fish of the trip.

With few exceptions these trout were all brightly hued, deep bodied, heavily spotted rainbows. In the time I was there I seldom hooked one of less than 13 inches. The few exceptions were darkly reddish-hued brown trout, just as stout, but not otherwise a match in size to the rainbows.

Bright Angel is not a large stream, averaging 30 to 40 feet in width and mainly shallow enough to require careful stalking to get within casting range of feeding fish. Its banks were not heavily brushed-in although some alders and willows lined it in spots. The average size of its fish, in comparison to the volume of water they inhabited, was quite surprising.

During the remainder of that and the ensuing two days I ranged up and down the red-walled canyon of the stream, from the Cottonwood Camp to its confluence with the mighty Colorado. The best fishing seemed to be near the mouth and where the smaller feeders of Ribbon, Phantom and Wall creeks ran into Bright Angel.

The secret of this stream is its relationship to the Colorado. The river's flow through the main canyon is regulated by the gates of the Glen Canyon Dam. Water coming from the bottom of Lake Powell provides a constantly cold, oxygenated flow in the river, even in the height of summer when the temperature at the canyon's bottom may climb to 120 degrees Fahrenheit. Because there are relatively few suitable feeder streams inside the Park, Bright Angel Creek gets a large number of the area's big spawners. I was there in midsummer but was told by one of the mule wranglers that the best time is in late fall or early winter when the spawners begin their run. I certainly had nothing to complain about. There were plenty of fish present and of an average size that would put many larger and more well-known streams to shame.

I didn't witness much mayfly activity while there; most of

the action being with caddis and various species of midge flies. At periods when no aquatic insect activity was apparent I had reasonable luck with hopper imitations and with small streamers, such as the Mickey Finn and Royal Coachman worked through the more broken water. It was challenging fishing in a marvelous "other-world" setting.

On my trip back out I chose to hike, breaking up the distance with an overnight stop at the Indian Garden Campground. Finally, pausing at the South Rim for one last look back into the canyon, I received a farewell salute from a garrulous long-tailed chat as he flew by me headed, perhaps, for the cooler recesses of the well-named Bright Angel Creek.

Chapter 25
POOLS OF MEMORY
The Long Hatch

The sun rose palely that morning, masked by smoky mists rising from the Targhee National Forest. Frost covered the riverside meadows, crunching like eggshells beneath the felt soles of our waders. It was late September and the valley cottonwoods were decked in their fall finery of gold. At ground level it was calm but high up, strong westerlies pushed rows of mare's tail cirrus across the sky.

You can say what you want about the fresh beauty of spring, the laid-back days of summer and the bright, clean white of winter but to my mind autumn is the grandest season of all, particularly in the realms of the northern brook trout and the western cutthroat. Then the forests and the fish are at the height of their coloring, insect hatches are still plentiful, fishermen comparatively few and the smells, tastes and sights of the stream courses are unmatched.

Having managed to simultaneously arrange a week of free time, fellow angler Greg Merrick and I had driven up to West Yellowstone from our Denver headquarters. We spent two days in the Park along the Firehole and the Yellowstone. I'm not sure how they work it presently but then the Park facilities were officially closed after Labor Day, yet access remained open. The only people we encountered were Rangers and other Park personnel cleaning up after the summer hordes and battening hatches for the coming winter. We saw no other anglers.

The day we fished the Yellowstone we parked off the main road about halfway between the Fishing Bridge and Buffalo Ford, hiking a quarter of a mile down a gentle lodgepole wooded slope to the river. The fishing was absolutely superb. We took one lemon-flanked cutthroat after another on Humpy dry flies.

While engrossed in this enjoyment we were unexpectedly hailed back to the bank by a Park Ranger. It seems that we were inadvertently fishing in a stretch of water closed during the entire season. However, he had watched us from the hill while we caught and gently released several trout and because we were keeping none, and there were no other people about, he told us to go ahead and enjoy ourselves, which we proceeded to do.

Following these delights we had driven west to Island Park, Idaho. Our first stop was at Will Godfrey's Fly Fishing Center but Will was off guiding somewhere. From there it was just a short hop to the upper fence line of Harriman's Railroad Ranch. Parking by the gate we slipped into our waders, strung up our rods and crunched our way across the quarter mile of meadow to reach the river.

The Henry's Fork, or North Fork of the Snake River, is at this point larger than the Madison, averaging about 300 feet in width through the ranch stretches. Its natural fertility and abundance of aquatic insect life made it one of the top two or three dry fly streams in the world and perhaps it is still ranked that high by some, although excessive publicity and the resulting fishing pressure have taken their toll.

The Railroad Ranch water was open to the public on a catch and release basis. Even back then, some 25 years ago, it was often crowded during the prolific midsummer hatches, especially during the weeks of salmonfly activity, but after Labor Day it became all but deserted except for occasional diehards like Greg and me.

It was about 8:00 a.m. when we reached the river and what a sight met our eyes. Clouds of pale, dancing mayflies filled the air alternately rising, then dipping, from tree top level nearer and nearer the water, whose surface was already speckled with thousands of flies laying eggs then, exhausted and dying, floating down with wings outstretched. Trout were rising everywhere, sipping in the spent dancers with reckless abandon.

For once I did not get carried away and make the mistake I often had in the past, assuming the insects' coloration without examining one closely. In trying to determine what free-rising trout are taking, often exclusively, one should not just watch the insects float by a few feet away. Closer examination may reveal that what looks like cream color may be pale yellow or what appears to be tan may be pale green or olive. During a heavy hatch such as this one the fish tend to be more selective than when foraging for odds and ends. The flies were of the family branch of *Ephemerella* known as pale morning duns but several species sport varying shades of body color. The ones we examined were of two colorations, pale yellow and light rusty brown; the latter we assumed were males. They could be matched by a size 16 artificial.

The pale morning dun is perhaps the single most important mayfly of western North America, being found in nearly all the streams of the Rockies and Cascades. The vast distribution of their races, plus population densities, plus the long seasonal range of their appearances combine to account for their importance. Some of the larger insects like the Salmonflies, Brown Drakes and Green Drakes get more publicity because of the monsters they can arouse but their emergences are often unpredictable and not nearly as long lasting.

Greg Merrick with his hands full on the Yellowstone River.

It would be high in the ranks of boredom to attempt a blow by blow account of our angling results that day. Suffice it to say that action was nearly continuous with fresh clouds of insects constantly emerging and the fish seemingly insatiable in their appetites for them. Several times I hooked, fought and released trout that were, quite literally, stuffed to the gills with flies.

Despite its width much of the Henry's Fork is not too deep and in many places it is possible to work across from one bank to the other without shipping water over wader tops. The bottom is easy going, mostly fine gravel lanes between the weedy channels. It is ideal water for the rather unorthodox method I prefer for fishing dry flies.

Since the 1850s dry fly anglers have been admonished by the experts to fish only upstream with the dry fly. This premise lasted unchallenged for years until a few upstart colonists began experimenting with alternatives. Notable among these was A. J. McClane, writing for *Field & Stream* in 1951. I had to agree with his views since I'd already been a heretic myself for 20 years.

As previously noted I learned to fly fish in the days of the $10 bamboo rod, the oiled silk fly line and the gut leader. In the early thirties when I began using dry flies I continued to fish with them as I had been doing with wet flies and streamers, working across and downstream to cover the water. It worked well for me then and I've never had cause to change the technique although I do in certain spots, especially in bright light and slow moving, smooth-surfaced water, fish up and across.

Drag has always been the greatest obstacle to successful dry fly presentation but I find that lazy S or slack line deliveries are easy to use and can often result in 15 to 20 feet of free float, which is plenty. Other advantages of the downstream technique are that the fly enters the fish's window of vision before the leader or line, there is less energy consumed in retrieving slack line, I don't have to cast over rising fish and downstream progress is a lot easier than bucking the current. Also, in mountain country there is often a strong downstream wind and, perhaps most important, the best fish lies often cannot be properly reached from below or even from directly across without drag or hang-ups. I'm speaking of jam piles, sweepers, stumps, the upper edge of cress beds, etc.

Proper line retrieval at the end of a float can be accomplished without alarming any fish present by using the rod to steer the line and leader to one side before lifting in the back cast.

Greg is normally an upstream dry fly caster but in the wide and not excessively deep runs of the Henry's Fork meadows the majority of both our deliveries were usually made across and

Admiring a nice cutthroat before release.

slightly down. Because trout lie in the weedy channels while feeding one can often work quite close to rising fish. The advantage of this lies not only in shorter, more controlled casting but also in more easily determining exactly what the fish are taking— nymphs, emergers, duns or spinners.

Big fish? Well, nothing over three pounds although Greg had

been surprised by one huge rainbow that quietly slurped in his floater from a corner along the grass-hung bank, then feeling the sting of the hook, methodically plowed upstream until the 7X tippet gave way. We both were close enough to see the trout and agreed that it had to weigh a minimum of six pounds. Greg bemoaned his loss until I corrected him with the admonition that old Isaak had given his angling companion: "Nay, the trout is not lost, for pray take notice no man can lose what he never had."

There were periods during the day when the dancers sat out a waltz or two. We then switched to size 18 Pheasant Tail nymphs or pale olive dubbed Gold Ribbed Hare's Ears. There were always a few observable adult flies over the water. Around 5:00 p.m., when we finally were surfeited and climbed out of the river, the PMD's were still emerging. I've never seen anything like it before or since. It had been the most perfect, matching the hatch, day-long action I've ever had the pleasure of experiencing and remembering.

Chapter 26

The Widow's Pool

Most fly fishing devotees I have known seem to be an odd mixture of reclusiveness and sociability. They like to go fishing with a companion or two but, in circumstances other than a float trip, usually prefer to fish apart. When not fishing they are most gregarious and chance meetings afield with friends are welcomed. This can lead to some interesting encounters.

As a case in point I had driven up from Colorado on a vacation trip, stopping off at intervals to fish the waters in the Wind River Range and the Tetons, several rivers in Yellowstone Park; eventually to wind up in Last Chance, Idaho, near the banks of the storied Henry's Fork.

Stopping in at Will Godfrey's Fly Fishing Shop for a visit I found myself in the midst of a small and somewhat hilarious get-together. In addition to Will, Ron Ferden and Mike Petrilli there was Bob Duncombe, at that time manager of the regional KOA Campground. Actually, his wife did most of the managing while Bob pursued more important lines.

During the course of conversation it was decided that we should celebrate our meeting with an overnight angling expedition. All hands were in favor. Where to go? Will came up with the answer. "Let's go back into the Centennial Valley," he suggested. "It's not far, there are a lot of trout, some big ones, and the scenery is great."

Bob, having also fished there, quickly seconded the motion and that was good enough for the rest of us. That evening we took off in a couple of pickup campers, heading back toward Yellowstone on Route 20. Just west of Henry's Lake a large sign by a graveled turn-off proclaimed it to be the gateway to the Centennial Valley and the Red Rocks National Wildfowl Refuge.

Winding northward through wooded hillsides for about 25 miles, we slowly gained elevation to the summit of Red Rocks Pass then quickly descended into the Centennial Valley, a huge long, wide bowl completely rimmed by mountains. Our destination was a cluster of three large spring-fed ponds near the eastern end of the valley. It was dark by the time we got there so we didn't fish that evening, opting for a quick meal of beans and wieners topped off with apple pie donated to the cause by Bob's wife. This was followed by a lengthy bull session around our small campfire. Sometime later we unrolled our sleeping bags and were lulled to the land of giant trout by the distant calls of geese and sandhill cranes

The sun got up early and so did we. Will had mentioned that the best fishing periods were between dawn and the time the sun rose high enough above the peaks to hit the water and again in the late afternoon when shadows began to lengthen.

We had parked near the edge of the largest body of water, Widgeon's Pond, sometimes called Picnic Pond. It was about five to six acres and contained brook trout, grayling, rainbow and cutthroat. The next largest in size was Culver Pond, also known as the Widow's Pool. A quarter of a mile long and averaging 150 feet in width, it contained only brook trout. The third, and smallest, pond was MacDonald's containing rainbow, some going to seven or eight pounds.

Widgeon Pond is so deep right up to the shoreline that it is best fished from a boat and with fast-sinking lines, neither of which we had with us, so we concentrated our efforts on MacDonald's and Culver. Both were wadeable, had heavy weed beds and were full of scud, fairy shrimp, backswimmers and other insect life.

We had a few exciting but futile encounters with the large MacDonald's rainbows. A size 18 Gold Ribbed Hare's Ear or other similar sized nymph on a 5X tippet was necessary to fool them but upon being hooked they would immediately dive into the thick

Ron Ferden battling a big brookie in the Widow's Pool.

weed beds and tear off. With the light terminal tackle needed it was nearly impossible to keep them from doing so.

We finally gave up on them and concentrated our efforts along the open banks of The Widow's Pool. Its brookies were fairly receptive to our offerings and a number of half pound to two pound fish were taken, the largest being a 19 inch, 3 1/2 pound male, whose lair I stumbled into. Although it was still midAugust these trout had already taken on their brilliant nuptial coloring.

Several fly patterns proved successful, the best one being a backswimmer imitation tied up by Godfrey which he called Win's Tan Fly.

During the period from 10:30 a.m. to 4:30 p.m. the bright weather kept the fish safely secreted in the weed growths and we spent the time exploring the huge valley, observing pronghorn antelope and mule deer and marvelling at its wetlands concentrations of ducks, geese, swans, cranes and shore birds.

The evening fishing was even better. The nearby sage covered slopes echoed with the whoops and calls of happy anglers as we traded comments on fish hooked and lost or landed and released. By agreement we kept just one trout each which formed the base of our evening meal cooked over the campfire coals. Then, somewhat reluctantly, we headed out over the Pass and back to Last Chance from where we went our separate ways.

Some of life's happiest periods seem to occur quite by accident and this had been one of those times—just the right combination of chance meeting, informal fellowship and an easy-going, pressure-less expedition with shared pleasures amid lovely surroundings.

It's the sort of memory that sticks with you.

Chapter 27

A Fine Art

I mentioned in the foreword that this was not to be another "how-to" book. However, to properly record my most memorable experiences I felt it imperative to include certain highlights of a little-publicized, but nevertheless prominent, phase of the angling craft. As Cervantes remarked, "There's no taking trout with dry breeches."

I can claim with some pride that falling in is an art I have studied all my angling life. Many unreasoning fishermen think of falling in as simply getting wet. Not so. When the proper grace and finesse are mastered there can be many precise variations of this theme, all truly magnificent in scope and virtuosity. Both before and after my cane days I have managed to fall into nearly every river I have fished and my stature as a seasoned performer is perhaps best characterized by my remorseless search for new fields to conquer.

Let's start with the simple forward and backward falls and then explore a few of the more complicated and graceful forms. The angler will do well to remember that in falling forward any element of clumsiness should be avoided. The basic tactic is to wade cheerfully upstream (or downstream) until the right foot can be placed firmly beneath an underwater root or similar obstruction. The fall forward should be executed quickly with both arms extended upright. A loud cry of "Aaaarghhh!" is optional but the entire body should be immersed, insuring that no dry articles of clothing remain. Further immersion can be accomplished by trying to retrieve the headgear or other accouterments being carried rapidly downstream.

The backward fall is quite similar except that it is triggered by the left heel being placed firmly upon the side of a round and algae-coated boulder.

Having mastered the basic forward and backward falls, the angler can then progress to the more complicated forms of immersion. Generally I find it best to reach a wader-high point toward the middle of the river and reserve the thrill of the actual maneuver until an attempt is made to retreat to the bank.

On Colorado's Blue River I achieved quite a rare form of the art by becoming completely soaked in a mere six inches of water.

Hard to do, you say? Yes indeed but being far from a neophyte in this art I succeeded splendidly, as follows: A good fish was rising under the opposite bank. The river was wide at this point with a strong tongue of current down the middle which would have created impossible drag. So I waded out. As I reached the central current I found myself among round, slippery rocks with about two inches of freeboard on my waders. Carefully I laid out line. The third cast fell right, there was a sudden boil and I struck. I dared not move but calling on all the skill and experience of many years I eventually brought to hand a lovely three pound brown. My back was turned toward my own bank and turning around was a nightmare; the strength of the current making it dangerous to lift a foot from the bottom. However, I managed it eventually and edged out of the current and into the stony shallows. I had taken a good fish under difficult conditions and hadn't even allowed a cupful into my waders so it was with a feeling of no small achievement that I strode out for the bank, only to encounter in mid stride an infinitesimal ridge of rock that effectively checked the forward movement of my feet. Not so the rest of my body which followed through quite beautifully. It was at this moment that I realized the truth of the statement that water will always take the line of least resistance—in this case down the neck of my shirt and on down to my socks. I had successfully completed the Forward One-Half Gainer, with complete saturation, in six seconds.

It may surprise some amateur anglers to know that the exercise of immersion can be carried out with its initial stage completely out of water. The most satisfactory approach is to walk to the edge of an attractive pool, placing the feet firmly upon a part of the bank that is suitably undercut by the current and then gaze hopefully out over the river.

Some years ago I achieved a notable performance of this Vertical Sink technique while fishing the Yellowstone River in Montana. The bank gave way, the water was deep and I was wearing chest waders. This is a beautiful and very graceful fall. You descend slowly into the water allowing plenty of time to throw away the rod and extend both arms to clutch at the bankside sagebrush; at the same time emitting a bloodcurdling yell. Provided the water level is sufficiently near the top of the bank you descend over the tops of the waders, allowing them to fill, which is most refreshing. Getting out again is difficult and exciting with the added spice of danger should the sagebrush you are clutching come out by the roots.

A variation of this fall can be found in the Vertical Collapse, wherein the fortunate angler suddenly disappears in a grass-covered beaver hole. Timing is important here as the collapse should be syncronized with the attention of one's companion being directed elsewhere so that upon receiving no answer to some idle comment he turns around, only to find empty space or at best a hat lying flush on the grass tops.

My research has led me to carefully observe the tactics of other anglers dabbling in this art and I have been privileged to witness several brilliant exhibitions. One of the finest was performed by my friend George, who confirmed his already versatile form by falling expertly through a small hole in a dock into eight feet of water. Although I examined him carefully, not a single article of dry clothing could be found. On the way back George made a shrewdly judged detour and, with impeccable timing, shattered the tip section of his bamboo rod with a stumble, followed by a karate foot stomp. I was full of admiration, knowing full well that I was observing one of the world's great performances.

On another, perhaps even more noteworthy occasion, George, in hopping about preparatory to sliding into his waders, accidentally stepped into a large and singularly fluid keepsake from a previous occupant of the streamside meadow. George rushed to the water to launder his sock. As he reached the edge he curled a deft toe under a stone and performed an exquisite variation of the Standing Forward Roll, entering headlong. This was achieved in what must be record time and in light conditions that were far from ideal. It makes one humble just to think about it.

Variations of the art can be practiced in still water as well as in rivers and often with the aid of props such as boats or docks. One magnificent form may be termed the Overwater Splits. This fall has one special advantage, in that it can be performed long before the fishing starts. To accomplish it you should keep one foot firmly on the dock and place the other on the edge of the boat. With any luck the boat will shoot off irretrievably into the lake. With a little skill you can supplement the ensuing crash into the water by splitting the midseam of your waders enroute.

Another particularly spectacular variation is the Off The Stern Gambit. This induced fall has been elevated to professional status by residents of Grayling, Michigan who regularly float the AuSable River. The idea is to wait until your boat partner is standing in the stern and facing away from you as he attempts to lay his fly up under a sweeper. The anchor is quietly lowered into the water and when the rope tightens in the current with a slight jolt, the standee demonstrates a neat parabola off into the river, normally accompanied by a large displacement of surface water. This gambit is particularly noteworthy in April or early May before the river has achieved any noticeable warming.

The Upwards-Down Fall, which is sometimes termed an Escalating Down Fall, is notable in that it is a completely dry fall. This occurs about midnight as you leave the waning rise to a flight of *Hexagenia limbata*. Crouching to observe, against the skyline, the tree marking the gate at the far end of the meadow you get your bearings and stride boldly forward, only to discover that the spine of a sleeping cow is knee-high to an angler. As you somersault over her she gets to her feet with a lurch and in so doing steps on your rod and/or anatomy. Game, set and match to the heifer.

I by no means have the space here to cover the multitude of variations but these few examples just might help any aspiring angler wishing to master this difficult but rewarding phase of the noble art of fly fishing. Remember that, as with anything else, practice makes perfect.

Chapter 28

The Far Side

I was blessed, or cursed, depending on your viewpoint with the Scots' epidemic of wandering. That, combined with my desire to test new and strange waters, has led to scores of major and minor fishing expeditions.

Charles Kuralt remarked in his charming volume, *A Life On the Road*, "All I know is that every traveler needs a carefree and optimistic spirit, curiosity about his surroundings, powers of keen observation—and a little bit of dumb luck." He might well have been specifically describing the peripatetic angler.

In 1975 I had resumed my marriage to Julia and had rejoined the Bear Archery Company as a special projects writer in their advertising department. The company had moved from Grayling, Michigan to Gainesville, Florida in 1978 and of course our family moved with them.

One of my assignments during this period was to work on a biography of my father-in-law, Fred Bear, which I finally completed in 1987, shortly before he passed away.

At the age of 70, a few months after Fred's death in 1988, I retired but continued to do freelance writing and to follow my pursuit of the angling muse, being greatly aided in this respect by a generous bequest from Fred.

So it was in my 73rd summer I found myself once again looking forward to a journey overseas in search of new fishing adventure. This time it was to be on the far side of the world in practically virgin waters—an almost unheard of situation in these civilized times and for no less than that royalty of the fly fisher's world, *salar* the leaper. Juliana Berners wrote back in the 17th century, "The moost stately fyssh that ony man may angle to in freshe water."

Bob Nauheim of Fishing International had contacted me at the beginning of the year with an intriguing tale of new and largely untested waters north of the Arctic Circle on the Finnish-Russian Kola Peninsula. It seems that the previous year, 1990, he had been in contact with Bill Davies and Monte Lewis of the Soviet Sports Connection, one of two groups authorized at that time to set up camps on the Kola rivers for fly fishing, a sport previously unknown to the region.

Large runs of Atlantic salmon were "discovered" by a few sportsmen in the Tersky region of the peninsula in 1989, an area that had previously been closed to outsiders because of its importance to the Soviet defense program. In 1989 Gorbachev's glasnost changed that and western sportsmen immediately took advantage of the new regime's openness by going into partnership with Russian sportsmen to establish fishing camps. There had been what they called guest fishing on three or four of the rivers in 1990, during which the Russian and American camp coordinators had ironed out most of the difficulties involved.

Bob was obviously excited over the prospects of being among the first to test these newly-found riches and when he said there was a vacant spot in the group going, I jumped at the chance.

This took place in January. We were scheduled to depart August 25. It was a long seven months to sweat out. Things went along smoothly; I finished building a new graphite rod for the occasion, tied a batch of flies, swam 30 laps five days a week to keep in shape and had sorted and resorted clothing and other necessities for the trip. Then, on August 18, all hell broke loose.

It was on that date that eight hard-line Communist officials in the KGB and military sent tanks and other troops into the heart of Moscow to overthrow Boris Yeltsin and his democratic followers and take over the government. Soviet President, Mikhail Gorbachev, had been arrested and held incommunicado in the Crimea. This was devastating news. We thought for sure that one of the results would be at least temporarily barred entry to all foreign tourists.

We had not realized the extent of the Russian peoples' newly found sense of freedom. Tens of thousands of their citizens rallied to Yeltsin's support, defying the tanks and other armed force units. They spent 48 hours (two long, rainy nights) effectively blocking access to their leader's sanctuary in the Russian Federation's Parliamentary Headquarters on the banks of the Moscow River. Much of the military sided with them.

In almost fairy tale fashion, the coup attempt completely collapsed on the third day. The hard-line junta members fled, only to be arrested, and Gorbachev was set free.

Unbelievable . . . we had run the gamut from high hope to despair to bright elation in just three days. If this sounds a bit self-centered, I hasten to add that we were certainly even more joyful for the Russian peoples' victorious stand and what it meant to them and all the rest of the world, than for the change of fortunes it meant in our infinitesimal but heartfelt case.

On Sunday, August 25, four of our group boarded an airliner at Kennedy Airport in New York for the eight hour flight overseas. We were to be joined in Leningrad by a Canadian and two of

Nauheim's friends from France, making our total expeditionary force seven in number.

After a short stop in Helsinki we transferred to a KLM 747 jet for the hour's flight across the Gulf of Finland to the historic city of Leningrad, cradle of three revolutions.

We were greeted at the terminal by Galina Mourina of the Soviet Sports Connection and Commerce Director for Soviet, British, American joint ventures. Galina should, in my opinion, be considered a national treasure. A dark-haired, dynamic, middle-aged Russian lady she has lived in Leningrad all her life, loves it, and was absolutely the best thing that happened to us on the entire trip. She expedited our way through the morass of customs, baggage facilities, etc., with a minimum of difficulties; then loaded us into a Mercedes bus for the hour's drive to and through the great city.

Leningrad, or Saint Petersburg as it was known originally, was founded by Peter the Great in 1703. From 1914 to 1924 it was known as Petrograd. During 900 days of siege by the German army in World War II the city lost two million, many by starvation, but held fast and triumphed in the end. It's population presently is approximately six million. While we were there, through public acclamation, the original name of Saint Petersburg was restored.

We checked in at the Astoria Hotel early in the afternoon and spent the rest of the day sightseeing via Galina's bus. Her intimate knowledge of the vast city proved invaluable. Many of the ancient buildings were huge, heavy walled, giant pillared with many still bearing visible scars of the World War II siege. Often the roof ramparts were lined with larger-than-life sized bronze statuaries of historical figures, and the interiors, especially of the cathedrals, were extremely ornate. On most of the larger buildings, interesting additions that could not have been more than a day or two old, were flowing banners of white over blue over red horizontal stripes—the flag of Russia designed long before by Tsar Peter the Great. The red and gold hammer and sickle emblem was not to be seen except in a few spots where it had been carved in the stone facade over or beside building entrances.

We visited most of the important landmarks such as the Summer and Winter Palaces, the Hermitage, Griffon Bridge, Peter and Paul Cathedral, Peter and Paul Fortress and many others but the one sight that impressed me the most was the bronze statuary groups in a huge square, dedicated to the memory of the brave defenders who died during the Nazi invasion. Just standing in contemplation before this great monument made my throat tighten and the hair on the back of my neck rise.

The streets were crowded with people, many hurrying to and fro on errands or standing in lines before an ice cream kiosk or a display of fresh fruits or vegetables that are trucked in daily from the countryside. The mood of the people seemed happy but subdued and a smile generally was met with a quick smile in return.

For a city of that size it was amazingly clean. The only signs of debris I saw were the remains of stone and timber barricades which had been erected in certain places against the possibility of tank incursions. Several times I observed rather elderly men and women sweeping boulevard curbsides with long handled brooms made, I believe, of birch boughs bound together.

One of our interesting stops was at an open-air market featuring mostly religious icons and art works, both photographic and painting. While there I purchased a set of the famous Russian Matryoshka nesting dolls carved from wood. This particular set was historical in that it featured replicas of Russian leaders, from an outer Gorbachev back to the innermost figure, a tiny Lenin. I paid $8.00 for the set. A month or two later, back home, I saw similar, but not as well done, sets advertised in an American import catalog for $249.00!

In the evening Galina took us into an older part of the city to a small Georgian restaurant where we enjoyed a simple but very adequate meal, highlighted by ceremonial toasts with their smooth but potent Boatka. The main dish consisted of small chunks of beef mixed with peas, carrots and new potatoes all in a highly spiced sauce and served in a small earthenware crock. There was also a fine salad of cabbage, tomatoes, cucumbers and onions, dark, sweet bread and ice cream for dessert.

We then returned to the Astoria and retired early as we had to rise at 5:00 a.m. the following morning to eat breakfast, check out and take the hour's ride to the airport.

We took off at 9:00 a.m. in a twin engine prop-jet, headed north across Lake Ladoga, the White Sea and the Arctic Circle on a two and a half hour flight to the town of Kirovsk. The countryside near Leningrad looks much like our midwest from the air, a flat or slightly rolling landscape marked by neat farm fields, a network of dirt surfaced roads and an occasional small settlement, usually situated along a watercourse.

As you proceed further north the terrain assumes an aspect more like that of northern Canada or interior Alaska. The forest here is known as the taiga, a boreal transition vegetation that spans the subarctic zone around the world, a link between the deciduous hardwood forests of the temperate zone and the Arctic tundra where no trees grow. The taiga is a forest of stunted evergreens, mainly spruce, fir and pine and dwarfed birch and poplars. Much of the forest floor is carpeted with the blond caribou lichen that needs a century to obtain its full growth, and which is the principal food of caribou in the western hemisphere and their blood relatives, the reindeer, here.

After a short wait at the Kirovsk airstrip, we boarded a large Aeroflot helicopter and in another hour landed near the Umba River camp. The Umba rises in a series of lakes and flows through rolling hill country to the White Sea, on the southern coast of the Kola Peninsula. Part of the peninsula is home to the semi-nomadic Sami Laplanders and their reindeer herds.

The camp was efficient and well-run for having been established just the previous year. An American, Herb Van Dyke, was the camp host and Soviet Sports Connection coordinator for all activities. The camp consisted mainly of a large cabin housing the kitchen, dining room and rooms for the guides to gather, tie flies, etc., a series of Quonset-like metal buildings used as sleeping quarters and two new cabins built earlier that summer. One of the latter became the quarters for me and the group member I was teamed with, Bob Sisson. It was very comfortable, with bunk beds, hot shower, chemical toilet, electric heater and lots of storage space.

In addition to Herb, the camp had a staff of river guides and several other Russian workers to do the cooking, serving and other camp chores. Food was simple but well prepared and very good. We had a lot of fresh, locally grown fruits such as apples, blueberries and raspberries and at every meal there were large pitchers of cooled juice made from these fruits. We had fresh eggs, pancakes, bacon and cereal in the morning and a variety of garden vegetables such as beets, cabbage, carrots, tomatoes, cucumbers, peas and onions for other meals. Meats were beef, pork and grayling. Desserts were cookies, pudding or ice cream.

The river itself is clear, picturesque and treacherous! It has the most unstable wading bottom I have ever encountered. The bed is lined with round-topped boulders of various sizes, all coated with a thin green alga that is slicker than bear grease. Spaces between the boulders catch and hold a wading staff (or my cane) in vise-like grips. The boot chains I had on my waders were all that stood between me and disaster—that and my ever-alert and watchful guide, Vitalè (Russian for Victor), who was constantly nearby to offer assistance. I fell only once and that not seriously—just enough to keep my reputation, as outlined in the previous chapter, intact.

Our guides spoke very little English although they knew more of our words than we did of Russian. I had a phrasebook along but most of the time, and especially while fishing, it was difficult to get at. We did much of our communicating with single words and sign language. The Russian word for "thank you" is pronounced "spaceebah." One of our group got it fixed in his mind that "thanks" in Russian was "placebo." Every time his guide would assist him in any way he'd loudly say "placebo!" and wonder why he got no response, such as a pazhaloostah (you're welcome). We corrected him a couple of times but he stuck to placebo, right to the end.

One of the larger holding pools was right in front of camp and rolling or jumping salmon were almost constantly in evidence there. Above camp there were long stretches of rapids with holding water just below and above. Not all of the holding lies can be reached by wading so we did some fishing from boats anchored in mid river channels.

Three miles upstream boat access ended at the junction of the Nizima and Krivets braids, whose rapids were shallow and boulder-strewn. From that point, hiking up a woods trail for another three miles brought one to a tent camp at the head of the Krivets fork. This stretch of the Umba offers magnificent diversity and proved to be the most productive.

The river there varies from 100 to 150 feet in width and consists mainly of swift water channels interspersed with bouldered pockets. A strong wader can cover much of this water with double-haul casting. I was of course somewhat limited in my approach but still had more good water to cover than time permitted.

The bordering woodlands were pristine and gorgeous. In addition to the ubiquitous fireweed, harebells and tag alder there was a profusion of blueberries, wild raspberries and a great variety of edible mushrooms.

We often lunched on the river banks and in midafternoon would pause for a break while the guides built a small fire and boiled water for tea. One day Vitalè wandered off into the woods during tea-time, returning 10 minutes later with a capful of mushrooms. He explained that in Russian these were called, "the mushroom that grows under birch trees." He cut some forked alder sticks and we toasted the mushrooms over the coals like marshmallows. Delicious.

Six of us spent the greater share of our stay at the upper tent camp because of the concentration of salmon in that area.

Despite the fact that we were considerably above the Arctic Circle the weather was unseasonably warm (it reached 85 degrees on September 1), the water was comparatively low and the anticipated early fall run of large salmon had not ascended the river. It was full of 10 to 15 pound fish from the earlier runs, which gave us plenty of action. There was only one large fish taken, that being a 40 pounder landed by Ewing Philbin. As he was fishing some distance from me at the time, and released the salmon, I did not get to see it but he later sent me a photo of it for my collection.

We found our hairwing fly patterns to be as productive as the more complicated and fully tied featherwing standards. In using hairwing flies, Col. Thompson's "The Patent" method of

A companion on Russia's Umba River battles salar the leaper.

presentation seemed to be the most deadly. This is a relatively simple procedure accomplished by casting at any angle across or slightly upstream, depending on the speed and depth of water being fished, and letting the lightly dressed fly swing around and down on a loose line, cruising freely in the current with no pull from the line. While the fly drifts beneath the surface the dressed line floats on top, making casting pick-ups easier. Because of the slack line used, which has to be tightened up before setting the hook, I seem to firmly hook a better percentage of taking fish with this method.

Umba River salmon fishing was set up as flies only and is also strictly catch and release. We kept no salmon and bent down the barbs on our hooks to facilitate release. There was no need to keep any for camp fare as the river was also loaded with large Arctic grayling (I caught one of 22 inches and over four pounds) that often intercepted our drifting salmon flies and were excellent table fish.

The idea of catch and release for salmon is questioned by some anglers. To me it makes good sense for, unlike the Pacific salmon species, *salar* does not die after spawning once but may go back to sea and return to the natal stream three or four times, the record being seven spawnings. As Lee Wulff used to emphasize, the Atlantic salmon is too valuable a game fish to be taken only once.

In some regions, Iceland for example, most salmon landed are kept, to be turned over to the landowner involved for the purpose of processing for food. As time goes on, however, and salmon stocks further decline, I feel the catch and release idea will become more and more accepted among anglers everywhere.

The first large pool below the Krivets camp, which someone had named Golden Pond, proved to be the most memorable for me. One afternoon I took four salmon there, from 12 to 15 pounds, with floating line and a size 6 Green Butt Black Bear and then let Bob Nauheim take over with the same pattern on a sinking line which resulted in three more. Two other excellent stretches were Long Pool and Captain's Pool but the wading was especially treacherous there. My usual wading progress was performed by shuffling along with a foot-dragging two-step, like a Sioux warrior dancing in preparation for the warpath. I had trouble reaching some of the best lies and made up a maxim to fit the occasion that goes like this: When your guide takes you to a favored salmon spot, no matter which side of the river you are on, it is always on the far side!

At any rate, the days passed all too quickly and it was soon time to depart. We fished right up to the last minute of the last morning and the helicopter plucked me right out of the edge of Long Pool—waders, fly rod and all. What I didn't know at the time was that Vitalè was to stay behind at the upper camp, and as a result I didn't get to wish him a proper farewell. I did leave one of my fly fishing outfits for him which hopefully he can put to good use. Despite the language barrier this 30 year-old Russian was one of the finest guides and riverside companions I've ever been privileged to know.

Our return flights to Kirovsk, then Leningrad, were uneventful but scenically interesting. Just after lifting off in the helicopter we watched a pair of reindeer swimming across the Umba not far from camp.

Arriving back at the Astoria in early afternoon we had the balance of the day for more sightseeing with Galina. In the evening we went to one of the old opera houses to see a stage production of *America, America,* with a troupe of Russian performers who had just recently returned from a tour in the United States. It was a most entertaining evening, a potpourri of chorus line and dance numbers, high wire feats, jugglers, single and group vocalists, magicians and comedians.

The following morning, after checking out and reclaiming our passports, we drove for the last time to the airline terminal and proceeded to spend a hectic hour or two trying to get ourselves and our luggage through customs, during the course of which I had one last interesting encounter.

Galina had spotted a lone unoccupied chair in a corner of the crowded room and, taking me by the arm over to it, she said to sit tight until I saw her wave to me. All around me were Russian men and women seated on chairs and benches waiting for I knew not what. Observing the ebb and flow of humanity I noticed a large orange and white cat slowly making its way through the forest of feet looking up into the faces of the seated people as it passed. It came to a stop in front of me, looked up at me briefly, then jumped up, curled into a ball on my lap and went to sleep; not moving until I finally saw Galina's signal and stood up. It must have sensed I was a sympathetic soul—Julia and I have always had a cat or two as part of our family.

On the return trip we stayed overnight in the Finnish capitol of Helsinki and spent the following day sightseeing. It is an almost antiseptically clean, bright city with many landscaped parks and monuments and is very easy to get around in due to their great trolley car network and the fact that nearly everyone there speaks English as a second language. We spent quite a bit of time in the harbor area roving around open air markets and browsing through the miles of aisles in Stockman's, one of the largest department stores in the world.

Our purchases were minimal for Helsinki is currently rated as the second most expensive city in the world to live in, Tokyo being number one. A hamburger in Helsinki costs $12.00! I bought six postcards which cost me $12.00 and the postage to send them to America was an additional $10.50. Nevertheless it was a most worthwhile stop and a great way to unwind from our bush trip. Another eight hours and we were in New York exchanging hasty "Good luck's" before scattering to catch connecting flights home.

The Kola Peninsula rivers were, until now, undiscovered waters from a fly fisherman's point of view. Their potential is enormous and with continued proper management the entire region holds a very bright future for the traveling angler. Helping pioneer this pristine fishing in a far-off land proved to be both a privilege and a thrill. For me it was a once-in-a-lifetime adventure.

The Stor Matte Pool

Afellow who spends a good share of his life pursuing trout and salmon will, if he fishes big water, sooner or later be struck with the sickening realization that he has hooked a fish that's too large for his tackle and for his skill. No matter when it happens one is always unprepared for it and the consequences are most often a morale-shattering experience.

A day on the Orkla River, Tuesday, July 2, 1992 at 4:05 p.m. to be exact, was my personal time of reckoning when a yard and a half of the river bottom detached itself to float up and engulf my infinitesimal size 2 Jock Scott.

I distinctly remember the sound of my guide's breath being sucked up in a great inhalation as the monstrous fish turned and sank back into the depths. After that everything seemed to have a dream-like quality and so it remains to this day.

Lee Wulff had long before impressed upon me the fact that most hooked salmon are lost in the first minute of play because they are struck or are held too hard. Knowing this, I held the bowed rod steady for some minutes before exerting further pressure hoping to lessen a bit of the fish's wildness and unpredictability.

When I did increase the arc of the rod very little happened—I might as well have been hooked to a log. Lee had taught me that once you do put heavy strain on the tackle it should be maintained, easing momentarily only when the fish makes a determined run or leaps clear of the water. Anglers are often accused of exaggerating when they tell of fish that escape but it is largely because big fish take longer to subdue and they are most likely to get off. Keeping only a light strain on the tackle will prolong the struggle and the longer the fight the more chance the hook has of becoming dislodged.

In this particular case, however, it was a moot point. The salmon was in complete control. When he did decide to move there was no question of stopping or turning him. Down the length of the dark pool he drove, leaping once before going through the bouldered chute at its foot and into the broad sweep of heavy currents below.

Glancing down, it was a distinct shock to see the bare metal of the reel spool through the few turns of backing left. I hadn't been in this dilemma since that night in Connor's Flats on the AuSable's South Branch (see Chapter 13). There was only one thing to do—give him the butt and hope things held together. I could not follow and doubted that he would stop so I tightened up on the line as fiercely as I could and just hung on. Not for long. With a loud "ping" the leader parted, nearly sending me over on my back from the sudden release of pressure. The great fish was gone. About 10 turns of backing were still on the reel. I felt rather lucky not to have lost the entire works.

When I regained my balance and had cranked in the backing and fly line I turned to my guide, Arne. "How large was he?" I asked.

"Eighteen, maybe 20 kilos," he solemnly replied.

Not one of you readers who is a fly fisherman needs me to record my feelings at that moment. The heavens were black, my heart was broken and the end of the world was at hand.

Hope springs eternal (as the poets declare) and so it must be for the angler. There are only two alternatives: give up the sport entirely or become permanently deranged.

The one basic rule of salmon fishing is patience, or perseverance, if you will. This entails two simple but absolute procedures. First, you must fish every cast as if you knew for certain it would be the one to raise a fish and second, resist striking until you feel the weight of the fish as he turns or if fishing with a dry fly until it disappears into the salmon's mouth. I learned this the hard way having lost more than one good fish through lack of self-discipline in tracking the fly or from improper timing in setting the hook. These are more important to the salmon angler than choice of fly pattern or positioning during its presentation.

I couldn't remain "down" too long. I was in the heartland, the dream country, of many salmon anglers. Scandinavia, and particularly Norway, has always been famous for its many fine rivers and gigantic salmon with fish to 50 pounds or more being taken nearly every season. The litany of her web of waterways rolls off the tongue like a recounting of Saints' names in the prayers of a Benedictine novitiate: the Laerdal, Stjordal, Driva, Alta, Maels, Tana, Vossa, Orkla, Arøy, Malselv, Namsen, Jolstra and nearly 90 more.

Sport fishing in Norway began in the 1800s after the Napoleanic Wars when travel throughout Europe became unrestricted. A few wealthy Britons and Scots explored the north countries and, finding incredible fishing, leased the fishing rights from the riparian landowners. This practice quickly spread and because of the expenses involved remained largely a rich man's diversion. This condition still exists although as my own case proves an angler of very modest means can experience its lure and tradition.

When I decided I had to wet a line in one or two of the storied rivers of Norway I first contacted a couple of the best-known sports travel agencies in the U.S. I knew they had fishing rights leases on some of the better salmon rivers. I found that it would cost anywhere from $6,000 to more than $10,000 per week, depending on which river one chose. Much too rich for my blood!

Having learned from experience elsewhere that riparian landowners hold the key to European fishing privileges and that hotels or inns located near rivers often had reserved stretches their guests could fish for a small daily fee, I contacted two Norwegian travel agents directly and found that by reserving inn space I could get on some of the best rivers for a fraction of what the U.S. agencies charged.

That did it. I signed up and six months later, with all reservations confirmed, I boarded a Scandinavian airliner. I left Newark at 12:00 noon on June 27 and arrived in Oslo eight hours later, but six hours earlier. It was like flying into tomorrow. That evening I boarded a train for a seven hour overnight run to Trondheim. Between napping on the overseas flight and a comfortable sleeping compartment on the train I was able to negate the effects of time-lag.

When I arrived in Oslo it was sunny and warm. The natives were complaining about a hot, dry summer, declaring there had been no rain for six weeks and the upcountry farmers were troubled. My arrival changed all that. By the time I arrived in Trondheim it was pouring rain and this continued almost steadily for the next seven days. This covered my entire stay at the Baardshaug Herregard Hotel in Orkanger, during which time I fished the Orkla River.

As defined by author Milford "Stanley" Poltroon the hallmark of fishing expertise is weather forecasting. For example, if it is going to rain a good fisherman stops by a dry goods store and purchases a raincoat, while the really expert angler goes into the nearest saloon and waits until it all blows over.

I attempted the latter ploy but finally had to concede defeat to the elements and ventured forth.

A large river, averaging a hundred yards in width, the Orkla was full of salmon and salmon fishermen. The latter were mainly Norwegians using oversize spinning tackle with 12 to 15 foot rods and heavy nine or 10 inch Rapala lures and spoons. I observed no other fly fishermen during my stay there. The spin fishermen could cover much more water than I could with my 9 foot graphite fly rod, number 8 sink-tip line and size 2 flies. Amazingly enough, there were very few fish being taken although they were constantly in evidence, porpoising and leaping. I had absolutely no action at all until I found the inn's most upstream beat about 20 kilometers south of Orkanger and above the tiny village of Meldal. Here the river was narrower, with forested banks and offering better wading coverage. This was the place of my undoing. The "Stor Matte Pool," Arne called it, translating to Big Trouble Pool.

It kept raining. I kept fishing. No more action. At the end of the week I boarded an Otter aircraft at the Vaernes airport in Trondheim for a 40 minute flight north to Namsos, where I was picked up and transported by van to the Overhalla Hotel in the village of Overhalla, near the mighty Namsen River.

It had rained right up until my departure from Trondheim. Now the skies were clear and the first sunshine I'd seen in a week brightened the scene. My optimism returned. The inn had great accommodations including an efficient wader drying room, indoor pool, sauna, excellent food and transportation to and from beats on the Namsen and Bjøra rivers any time of the day or night.

The Namsen proved a problem. A very large river, it averages 200 to 300 yards across, in places widening to nearly a quarter of a mile. Most of its best holding water is among the center currents and cannot be reached from shore by the threadliners, let alone by fly fishermen, even those with long two-handed rods. There are a couple of stretches where the best lies can be covered by wading. That is where I spent most of my time although I did spend eight hours one day fishing from a boat. This is generally done by trolling the lure or fly while the ghillie constantly rows back and forth over the favored holding areas—termed harling. I chose to cast rather than troll the fly but had not a single response for my efforts. I tried tube flies and many standard patterns on floating, sink-tip and full sinking lines. Nothing.

The morning after my arrival I awoke to more moisture. Lowering clouds were full of rain and getting rid of it as fast as they could. This condition let up only rarely during the ensuing week. To add to the general dampness I managed to become totally submerged one morning while waist-deep in the Namsen's currents, thus updating my long and enviable record (see Chapter 27). A round boulder rolled under my foot and over I went. Thanks to the inn's efficient drying room, however, I was back in business with all dry gear in just four hours.

I fished on. The rains continued. No action from the fish. Then I found the Bjøra. This is a short river, the outlet of a large lake from where it winds some 10 to 15 kilometers before emptying into the Namsen below the village of Skogmo. A much more friendly river than the overpowering Namsen, the Bjøra is characterized by very deep, dark bends, extremely clear water and bars from which most of the water can be covered by wading and use of the double-haul. The banks are lined with Queen Ann's lace and witches' tears (the Norwegian name for purple fireweed) and green belts of birch, pine and spruce spreading back toward the

A fine Bjøra River salmon.

more open, rolling farm country. Even while fishing in the rain, with cool breezes whispering ancient songs in the gnarled pines above, I felt a wonderful sense of tranquillity and solitude. During the four days I fished there I encountered no other fishermen.

The Bjøra responded with three lovely salmon of five, seven and 10 kilos, all bright silver fresh-run fish. All were taken on a size 2 Thunder & Lightning hairwing fly. It would be nice to wind up this account with a tale of hooking and landing another fish like the first one encountered in Stor Matte but it just didn't happen.

When the second week ended I flew south to the ancient Hanseatic port of Bergen and from there took prearranged tours by bus and ferry through the magnificent fjord country. Norway has a coastline of 1,250 miles. Mountains and fjords dominate the landscape. Many of these long arms of the sea penetrate the land mass for many miles, can be two or three miles wide and some reach two-thirds of a mile in depth. Nearly every arm of every fjord has a salmon river emptying into it.

The rains continued through my week of fjord touring but they could not detract from the wonderful vistas. There were let-ups during which I managed to do some photography.

In my travels two strong impressions stood out. Even in the most precipitous reaches where mountain slopes were nearly vertical any ledge or bench that leveled out enough to support one held a dwelling place. Often these small homesteads, perched high in tiny clearings like raptors' aeries, could be reached only by foot trails. Many of the locations I observed were absolutely amazing in their seemingly total isolation from the world thousands of feet below.

My second impression was even stronger. During the three weeks of my stay I covered quite a bit of terrain and never once observed any old car bodies, rusting or abandoned farm equipment or other cast-off bric-a-brac. There was just no such unsightly litter. I hadn't seen such a clean, green landscape since traveling through Nova Scotia. The Norwegians are proud of their beautiful country, and it shows.

The fjords were all spectacular especially those having narrow arms cutting into the heart of the mountains, like veins of black slate set in a matrix of green. The Sogne, Nord, Hardanger and Geiranger fjords are outstanding in their scenic appeal, especially the latter with its many hanging waterfalls dropping thousands of feet down sheer rock walls and the inviting little village at its head, which I couldn't help comparing to a Disney World theme park—except this was for real.

My tour ended back in Oslo with a very pleasant visit at the home of the Roe family, Jon, Gladys and Eric, who are distant relatives on my wife's side of the family.

Despite the rather poor fishing results it had been a really worthwhile trip. The sport was good, the scenery grand, the people friendly and almost everyone spoke English. It is only fair to add that the record salmon one hears about are really few and far between. One should not be lured to Norway solely for that quest. Even without the fishing this land of the Vikings is one of the most magnificent areas on our planet—even in the rain. My memories of it are strong, with of course the strongest being the afternoon when I met my Waterloo at the foot of the Stor Matte Pool.

The Pools of Oz

When Julia and I moved to Florida with the Bear Archery Company in 1978 two of the finest new friends we made were Ron and Gretchen Olberding. Both were originally from Nebraska. Ron was a lawyer and having been brought up in a rural atmosphere, was a hunter and angler like myself. Neither of them was really happy with either the Florida terrain or the type of cases Ron was handling in court. In 1983 he received an offer to serve as a Circuit Judge in their home state and he and Gretchen and their two teenaged sons, Lewis and Mathew, lost no time in making the move back west. Their new base of operations was a neat farmstead outside the small town of Burwell.

The terrain in that section of northcentral Nebraska is known as the Sand Hills country, mostly flat or gently rolling prairie land. Traveling across it on the highways one is struck by the monotony of the landscape: mile after mile of ranchlands with few stands of trees except those in the occasional farming communities. Appearances, as mother taught, can often be deceiving. We kept in touch and a year or so later Ron invited me out to pursue my favorite pastime; stalking the wily trout.

"Trout fishing on the prairie?" I asked, "What is it, a stocked farm pond?"

"Nope," replied Ron, "It's river fishing with heavy hatches and large fish. Don't knock it 'til you've tried it."

I thought surely he must be exaggerating but was intrigued. The following April I drove to Boise, Idaho on business and on the return trip, early in May, I stopped in Burwell for a visit.

"Well, it's too early for the big dry fly hatches yet," explained Ron, "but the stream seldom becomes too high and roily. We should be able to get a few nice fish."

Early the following morning we left Burwell, driving north to Bassett, then west to Valentine, then southwest across the Niobrara River. Along the way Ron filled me in on the background of the area. His brother-in-law, Dr. Cleve Trimble, owns a cattle ranch through which the river we were to fish runs. The river has its beginnings in springs issuing from eastern-facing slopes in the wildest part of Cherry County. It runs due east for some 60 miles, flows into Merritt Reservoir then runs to the north about 15 or 20 miles before emptying into the Niobrara. Its entire length flows through isolated and private ranchlands; there is no public water on the river. It does not flow past or near towns or highways and because of its isolation is little known, even to state residents. Cleve's spread lies along its lower reaches between the reservoir and the Niobrara. Because of the prairie rattlers occasionally encountered along its rims, it is called Snake River.

That first trip in to the Trimble Ranch was a real revelation. In late afternoon when Ron stopped to unlock the gate leading into the ranchlands I noticed a line of green pines in the distance, standing stiff and silent like soldiers at parade rest. As we drove on the pine ramparts became more and more distinctly detailed. Finally Ron parked and we walked the last few yards to the trees. Without warning the ground dropped off before us into a thousand foot deep canyon. It was steep-sided and heavily wooded but between gaps in the trees the silver thread of a sizable watercourse could be glimpsed. The melody of its waters drifted up to us from far below while overhead a redtailed hawk screamed annoyance at our invasion of his realm.

After a night spent at the ranchhouse we breakfasted on bacon and eggs, got our tackle in order then drove the short distance to the canyon. The redtailed hawk was back, hanging in the azure sky like a winged ghost, fingering the currents of rising air through its primaries. As I watched, it slid down, etched against the dark slope of the canyon's western rim. Suddenly dropping faster, legs extended and wings braking, it evaporated into the tall grasses among the pines. It too had found breakfast.

Snake River Canyon.

From the rim we made our way down the slopes over a sandy, rutted and steep trail road, passable only with a four-wheel drive vehicle such as Ron's. To me the sudden transition of descent into the canyon from flat prairie through lovely wooded glades was almost unreal, as if a tornado had picked us up and deposited us in the kingdom of Oz. Just dropping over the edge in these surroundings has the uncanny ability to bring on a sudden sense of relaxed separation from the world above. This feeling never left me during all the time spent in the canyon and always returned on subsequent visits. It is enhanced by frequent sightings of grouse, wild turkeys, whitetail and mule deer and by the timbered, high-walled ramparts marking isolation from the open, wind-swept plain.

The river itself is, by my standards, just about perfect. Averaging 50 to 75 feet in width, it is one long curving succession of sparkling riffles, runs and pools. Its sand and graveled bed is readily wadeable and from midstream short casts can direct the fly to any pocket or lie along either bank. The bottom is liberally inhabited with the aquatic larvae of mayflies, caddis, stoneflies and lesser insect forms. Despite the cool air and water temperatures of this early season and the obvious lack of surface activity, a weighted stonefly nymph pattern drifted along the bottom furnished enough action to please any angler.

The Snake River's trout are not piddlers. Rainbows and browns, they average over a pound in weight. The majority of fish I landed and released were two and a half to four pounds and in excellent condition.

On this particular day we spent some time sitting on the grassy bank just watching the water and the antics of a belted kingfisher. Many fishermen I know are always too busy fishing to look around and see where the hell they are. That's what I like about companions like Ron. He takes time to smell the flowers, listen to the bird songs and watch the flight of a magpie or raven.

We were rigged and ready though, and after a bit, still from my sitting position, I flipped a cast out over the three foot depth of water in front of us. Before the nymph had sunk more than a few inches a good trout charged up at it, nearly driving the kingfisher perched nearby into hysterics.

The fish was nicked and would not come to the fly again but that broke our static spell. I started upstream while Ron ventured down, after setting a time to meet in late afternoon and agreeing to each keep one trout for our evening meal. Despite the culinary success of the ensuing repast, the two pound rainbow I kept for that purpose was the only fish I have permanently removed from its home in a canyon pool. On subsequent trips neither of us has kept any, preferring to catch and release.

I have not yet taken a fish there of less than a pound. Four pounds is my largest Snake River trout to date (a heavy, hook-jawed male rainbow) but there are much larger trout in residence. My one trouble is that on each of the three trips I've made there it was either too early or too late in the season for the best fishing.

One of these years I'm going to get there at the right time, during the big hatches of midsummer and maybe, just maybe, hook the kind of lunker that dampens the inside of your waders.

One of the greatest double assets I presently have as a fly fisherman is a lifetime invitation from Cleve to visit there anytime I wish, plus the ready and able companionship of Ron. In this day and age it is better than money in the bank.

Chapter 31

Heartland

Throughout our country the more publicized waters have been exploited for some time and the situation gets worse each year. There is still good fishing to be found on many of our rivers but for me the pleasures of angling are considerably lessened by having to fight through throngs of people for a place to wet a line.

For this reason I do not fish the big waters much anymore, preferring the intimacy and quietude of smaller streams away from the crowds.

Three of my favorite fishing spots in the West are close to heavily trafficked waters, yet are comparatively unknown because their entire courses flow through private posted property. Two of these are feeder streams of Montana's Big Hole River, which to this date contain the largest Montana grayling I know of, plus some of the finest brook trout fishing in flowing water left in the U.S. The third is the lovely little river in Nebraska, described in the previous chapter, whose entire length is, again, through private ranchlands and thus largely unknown. It yields better fishing for large rainbows and browns than any other western river I know of, including such giants as the Yellowstone, Madison, Henry's Fork and the Missouri.

Aside from these exceptions my favorite area for present-day trout fishing lies within the vast reaches of Wyoming's Wind River Range.

The jagged backbone of these mountains forms part of the Continental Divide; its eastern watersheds feeding the Wind River (see Chapter 22) while the Green River basin drains the western side. After having fished many of the "glamour" spots in the fly angler's world, I still believe that the beauty and lure of this Rocky Mountain wilderness cannot be beaten.

The 2.4 million acre Shoshone National Forest covers most of the range, encompassing the Bridger Wilderness Area, the Wind River Indian Reservation and the Glacier and Popo Agie Primitive Areas. Within this region are 4,000 lakes and more than 800 miles of streams. All ORV's and ATV's are excluded from these wilderness and primitive areas; the only allowable passage being by horseback or hiking. Thus the region offers one of the very few remaining combinations of lovely alpine wilderness and a myriad of angling opportunities. The territory is heavily used in summer by hikers and climbers but solitude is not too difficult to find.

Although the Green River is a major tributary of the mighty Colorado River system it is not nearly so well-known among non-residents as other major Rocky Mountain rivers. The Green rises in the heart of the Wind River Range below Gannet Peak; at 13,000 feet, Wyoming's highest mountain. Snow melt from the 12,000 foot Mammoth Glacier forms Wells Creek, a principal source of the Green River that, fed by many other tributaries along the way, courses through a deep 12 mile canyon, through the Green River Lakes and past Squaretop Mountain into a broad valley through Fontinelle Reservoir. It then meanders a hundred miles south through Utah's Flaming Gorge and eventually, some 730 miles from its source, feeds the Colorado on its journey to the Gulf of California.

The 502 foot high Flaming Gorge Dam that backs the Green River into a 90 mile lake provides good fishing above, and even better below, through spectacular Flaming Gorge and Red Canyon, carved by the river as it passes through the Uintah Mountains.

This is some of the finest tail water trout fishing in the United States. Twenty thousand rainbow, cutthroat, brown and brook trout have been counted by electroshocking in the first mile of river below the dam. Seven miles downriver at Little Hole, a take-out point for floaters, there are 13,000 to 17,000 trout per mile. The following nine miles of river downstream to Indian Crossing in Brown's Park are just as good. Both float trip and wading (or preferably a combination of the two) can be productive for sizable trout. The one bug in the ointment is the very heavy river traffic common throughout these lower waters.

Although I've fished there several times, usually by driving in from Craig, Colorado over Route 318 through the Hole-in-the-Wall country (an old hideout of Butch Cassidy and the Sundance Kid), I prefer the upper Wind River Range reaches of the Green to the lower and larger waters of the Uintahs.

The town of Pinedale at the western foot of the range is justly famous among anglers for being the gateway to the New Fork and Green rivers. There are literally thousands of miles of streams that feed their drainages, all of which contain some kind of trout. Those easy to get to are somewhat spoiled by overfishing but if you venture far enough off the most popular paths you can still strike it rich. This is especially true after Labor Day.

Much of the wilderness is even without trails but can be explored by those willing to travel by topo map and compass. Because of crowding on the larger and more well-known waters, I

A typical heartland mountain stream.

now seek out the headwater streams and lakelets where the fish may be small but the surroundings and comparative solitude are the real trophies to be gained; and where I can keep a couple of trout for an enjoyable campfire meal without feeling guilty. Deep pools and beaver impoundments along the Green's tributary creeks, such as the Big Twin, Wagon, Piney, Rock and Horse, offer good sport as do untold numbers of lesser-known waters further back in the range. I've been temporarily "turned around" in there more than once but as that ultimate outdoorsman, Nessmuk, observed: "If you don't care where you are, you ain't lost."

I don't like to get too serious about my fishing and in such surroundings often prefer a slow pace. I'm inclined to be dreamy (lazy?) and enjoy watching the streamside coverts for birds or other animals, the changing cloud patterns and the play of light and shadow on the water. Spotting an ouzel or raptor I'll stop fishing altogether while I can watch its fascinating pursuits. For me this is all a fine and necessary part of being there.

This is the continental heartland I now visit again and again, as long as I am able. Traversing these headwater tracts I often think of the old mountain men who, with the Shoshones, were the first to explore here. Their goals were the tiny streams high up as are mine—they after plew, I after native trout; their tools the flintlock and traps, mine the pack rod and flies. Yes, times have changed but in a few wonderful places the scenes, sounds and scents remain as they were a hundred years ago. There, the catch is always more than trout.

Perhaps next summer if you happen to be in that region and run into a slightly stooped, gray bearded old-timer using a cane as a wading staff, we may meet and exchange pleasantries common to the fly fishing fraternity.

Chapter 32

The Best Revenge

I had not been back in one of my favorite western fishing areas, the Wind River Range, for a number of years. Following my 75th birthday in June, 1993 I suddenly decided that a great way to celebrate my three quarters of a century would be to venture once again into the roadless tracts of the Shoshone Indian Reservation.

Driving to Ft. Washakie I secured the necessary tribal fishing permit then drove west over the foothills on the Sage Creek road that ended, after a rough, rocky 18 miles, at the St. Lawrence Basin Ranger Station. There was also a Shoshone horse packers' camp set up in the basin. The Indians had established a guiding business and for a $250 per horse fee they take visitors into the high country and either stay with them or operate on a drop-off and pick-up later arrangement.

This was tempting but it wasn't for me. This time, despite my somewhat bent frame and the double load of years and backpack, I was determined to make it as far as I could on my own. Like Nessmuk or Muir I traveled light. In my internal frame pack was a mummy type down sleeping bag, a ground cloth (space blanket), light nylon tarp, one burner propane stove, small water purifier, change of underwear and socks, toilet and first aid articles, a supply of freeze-dried food packets and my 7 foot takedown trout rod and reel, box of flies and camera. Total weight was about 45 pounds.

After parking the faithful Toyota in the shade and disconnecting the battery cables to preserve its juice I set out on the South Fork Trail, heading west toward the Continental Divide. Knowing it would be uphill going most of the way I set a slow but steady pace with frequent stops to admire the surrounding forest and inhale deep drafts of the cool air. There's no trouble in getting a lung full of clean air in that country and it goes to the head like a double shot of Old Stumpblower.

I was following the same route I had traversed years before and each new vista that opened up was fresh, yet familiar. The first day I went just five or six miles stopping at the head of the Meadows, short of Windy Ridge, in midafternoon to make early camp and rest. It would be another day to the nearest fishing opportunities.

Making camp was a simple procedure. It began with clearing a spot of cones, twigs, etc. for my sleeping bag, scooping shallow depressions at the shoulder and hip locations and filling them with pine straw or dead grass, laying down the ground cloth then the bag, erecting the nylon rain fly overhead with tie cords, assembling rocks for a small fireplace, cutting a stick to support the tea kettle, gathering twigs and dry branches for a fire and heating water to reconstitute a freeze-dried food packet and for tea. The rain fly proved superfluous as the weather remained clear and I did not bother to put it up again the rest of the trip.

Having eaten I sat quietly back and in the silence of the forest listened to things beyond the clamor of urban man. Setting sun and crimson clouds were a part of the silence where the ancient gnarled spruce and pines were my only overnight companions.

The next morning, after a breakfast of reconstituted cheese omelet and strong black tea, I assembled my pack and took off up over the bouldery saddle of Windy Ridge then down its wild-flower spangled western slopes to the Entigo and Wilson Creek drainages. Turning south I hiked to Raft Lake to make camp. I was now 13 miles in from the St. Lawrence Basin.

The number of backpackers met along the trail was surprising. Twenty years before it had been rare to run into anyone at all in this area, yet now the trails were quite heavily used with of course the added traffic of occasional pack trains of from two to six people and their Shoshone guide. Many of the backpackers I met were young people and some carried packs that I probably couldn't have lifted to my shoulders. Most who had fishing tackle carried spinfishing gear—I met very few fly fishermen. All those with whom I passed the time of day seemed appreciative of their surroundings and I was later happy to note the lack of litter at various campsites and along the trails.

The small but fierce mountain mosquitoes were out in force so I lit up a short black Parodi cigar, one of my holdovers from days at Frenchman's Pond and the best bug repellent there is. Because they're rock-hard to begin with they always seem fresh no matter how long they've been stored in a fishing vest.

Raft Lake yielded a brace of plump cutthroat trout—pure ambrosia when wrapped in foil and roasted among the coals of the campfire. The Wind River peaks and the small lakes near their base were now within three or four miles.

As I prepared to retire the hoot of a barred owl came like a ghost from the dark woods and faded in the murmur of wind through the treetops. Hearing him I was reminded of the ancient adage, "and owls that mark the setting sun declare a starlight evening and a morning fair." This was confirmed the following dawn when the sun rose through a cool but cloudless sky. Another perfect day.

I lay abed listening to a distant coyote chorus until the sun was high before breakfasting and leisurely hitting the trail up the North Fork of the Little Wind River, past several small lakes, to Wykee Lake. I spent a couple of enjoyable hours fishing there, releasing several nice cutthroat, then continued up the trail from its inlet to the south end of my ultimate destination, Sonnicant Lake. Its lovely glacier-carved bowl lies right at the eastern foot of the Continental Divide at an elevation of something over 10,000 feet. It holds mainly brook trout although there are also a few large cutthroat present.

There were signs of recent campers, yet fortunately none were about during the few idyllic days I spent in the area. I set up my camp in a secretive spot back from the lake near a small spring. Although it was early August snow banks still lay here and there among the groves, furnishing overnight refrigeration for trout intended for breakfast.

Twenty years before I had taken 18 to 20 inch brookies from this water but easy as it proved to catch all the fish I wanted to eat, none were over 12 to 14 inches.

Mornings here were still and fine, though quite brisk. Lakeside grasses were often rimmed with hoarfrost and tiny shards of ice glinted along the shoreline. At such times fishing was best if I waited until nearly noon when the sun was high enough to warm things up.

One morning, in a pool below the small falls at the lake's outlet, I spotted a huge cutthroat. I was using my floating line and a dry fly at the time. Circling around to get below the fish I lengthened line with false casts then set the fly down a couple feet above him. The fly settled like thistledown, floated over the trout like thistledown and like thistledown was ignored. Two more drifts brought similar results: seemingly good delivery and drag-free float but to no avail.

"Well," I said to myself (like all experienced anglers when alone I constantly converse with myself), "if he won't take that, maybe a terrestrial would be more to his liking."

I replaced the Humpy with a Flying Ant, put a bit of floatant on it and cast it in the same fashion. It had scarcely touched the water before he had it and the ensuing foam-churning epic battle raged up the pool, and down into the next, and the one below that. Everything held and finally the 22 inch cutthroat lay quietly in my hand, its gills flaring slowly in irregular rhythm. Lowering him below the surface, head facing upstream, I gently moved him back and forth to help him take in oxygen. The gill action steadied and finally, with a slow, dignified sweep of his tail, he eased back into the depths of the pool. A good fish and a great memory.

The fish I kept for eating were the 10 to 12 inch brookies—in my opinion one of the greatest culinary delights known to man. A week of leisurely hiking and fishing in various small lakes and connecting streams passed. Finally, having tired somewhat of eating fish and running low on other supplies, I decided it was time to retrace my steps.

The following night, my last alone in the wilderness, was spent near Raft Lake. That evening, although the embers of my final campfire were dying the glow in my heart kindled anew as dusk crept in with its sudden charm, calling forth the spirits of remembrance. The spell of clear mountain air laden with the fragrance of evergreens and carrying the murmur of a brook mingled with the calling of ravens somewhere just out of sight drifted through the surrounding glens and glades.

Tomorrow I would be back in the world of man. Whatever happens from here on can never dim nor erase my memories of these and other trails through the real world of nature's realm. In a world hell-bent on developing itself to death fly fishing, while it lasts, is for me, the best revenge.

Chapter 33

POOLS OF MEMORY

Frenchman's Pond

J ohn D. Voelker, better known to hosts of readers under his pen name of Robert Traver, was one of the finest men I ever knew. Although he probably never realized it I greatly admired and respected John, much as I would an older brother or favorite uncle. For me his passing marked the end of an era.

John was born in Ishpeming, Michigan on June 29, 1903. Until he died in the early spring of 1991 he headquartered for the better part of his life in the same house on Deer Lake Road in which he was born.

Following a youth spent knocking around the Upper Peninsula, mainly aboard various iron ore freighters, and along the trouty reaches of the Yellow Dog, Big Dead, Fox, Mulligan, Whitefish, Two Heart, Ontanogon and Escanaba rivers John decided to forsake the pursuit of his favorite quarry, the brook trout, long enough to study law. He attended Northern Michigan College in Marquette then went on to get his law degree from the University of Michigan in Ann Arbor. After passing his bar exam he married a girl named Grace who lived near Chicago and went to work for a law firm in that city. He sorely missed the north woods and its clear streams and in a few years persuaded Grace to move back to the Upper Peninsula, where he began a variegated life as a backwoods lawyer in Marquette County.

John served for 14 years as District Attorney of his home bailiwick then continued as a Defense Attorney. It was during the long U.P. winters that he began to write novels.

His first book, *Troubleshooter,* was published in 1943 and rapidly became a best-seller. John had a positive knack for relating adventures involving colorful regional characters and folklore, laced throughout with his own special wry humor.

Other Traver books drawn from his life as backwoods lawyer and angler were: *Danny And The Boys* in 1951; *Small Town D.A.* in 1954; *Trout Madness* in 1960; *Hornstein's Boy* in 1962; *Anatomy of a Fisherman* in 1964; *Laughing Whitefish* in 1965; *The Jealous Mistress* in 1967; *Trout Magic* in 1974 and *People Versus Kirk* in 1981.

Most of these books are based on his experiences during the

Marquette County lawyer period and the tales they tell are as authentic as they are hilarious. Many are taken by the average reader as flights of fancy but were actually true incidents or based on truth, with perhaps just a bit of John's descriptive embellishment.

The characters John wrote about were for the most part real, only the names being changed or altered. Timmy Pascoe was really Tommy Cole. Danny McGinnis was really Dan Spencer. One of these early contemporaries in particular requires further mention as he played a basic role as John's friend and character molder.

Tommy Cole was another of the same breed as John. I knew him from the time I was a youngster in high school. He and my cousin, Redge Moll, had grown up together, gone through World War I together and remained close friends for as long as they lived. Tommy had been gassed during the war and lived mainly on a disability pension although he did hold jobs as chauffeur for Redge's father, Dr. Moll, as Field Biologist in the Seney Wildlife Refuge and later as caretaker for the Cleveland Cliffs Iron Company's Silver Lake hydro dam near the headwaters of Big Dead River.

Tommy's avowed declaration upon returning from overseas was, "I ain't never going to punch a damn time clock again," and he never did. As John once said of Tommy, "This man lived like a human being was meant to." He obviously believed it for he ended on the same trail.

Tommy Cole was a true artist with the fly rod and was the instigator who got John Voelker hooked on that phase of the sport. Under his tutelage, John became strictly a fly angler and ever afterwards scornfully referred to bait rods as "girders" or "derricks" and to worms or other live bait as "pork chops."

Later, in 1935, Tommy and Redge took me under their wing and, in addition to fly fishing, taught me the art of fly tying as well. I fished many times with all of them while still a brash neophyte. At that time the Eastern brook trout was still the ruling resident of the U.P.'s many streams, ponds and beaver creeks and these speckled beauties were our principal quarry.

Tommy Cole passed away in the late 1960s but his conversional work still bears fruit in the efforts of his disciples. John never forgot Tommy and held his memory ever-fresh for the rest of his life, as will I. Changing times nearly insure there will never again be men of their intrinsic anomaly.

After having been elected as District Attorney for Marquette County and serving in that capacity John was appointed to the Supreme Court of Michigan during the term of Governor G. Mennen Williams in 1957. He was re-elected twice and wrote more than a hundred legal decisions. In 1958 his book, *Anatomy of a Murder*, based on Voelker's real-life defense of a murder case, was published and quickly gained fame. It was a Book-of-the-Month Club selection and on the best-seller lists for more than a year. Not long after, the movie rights were purchased by MGM Studios, the film being directed by Otto Preminger, shot on location in Marquette County and starring James Stewart and Joseph W. Welch, the judge who had previously been a prominent figure in the McCarthy hearings.

This marked the turning point in John's life. In 1960 he proceeded to do what few men have the courage to do and dropped out of the big city rat-race. He had read Thoreau, "There is no more fatal blunderer than he who consumes the greater part of his life getting a living," and Robert Lewis Stevenson, "It is not by any means certain that a man's business is the most important thing he has to do," and firmly believed what they had written. John resigned his position as State Supreme Court Justice and moved back up to his ancestral home in Ishpeming. From then on he did what he really wanted to and what so many others have dreamed of. Except for special trips he lived in his beloved north woods year-round, writing novels and feature magazine articles during the winter and angling for his lovely brookies in the summer.

Following his retirement to the U.P. John may have been thought of by some as a recluse but he certainly was not. For years he continued to travel widely at intervals even though he preferred the serene, unhurried pace of life in Lake Superior country. He also had a cottage on Lake Charlevoix where he occasionally spent weekends with family members, ". . . In the interests of domestic tranquillity," as he put it.

John firmly believed that Mother Nature's three noblest creations were the ruffed grouse, the whitetail deer and the Eastern brook trout. Fly fishing for the latter was as necessary to him as breathing. He once wrote: "Trout fishing is so enjoyable, it should be done in bed."

Anyone puzzled over John's belief should carefully read his famous *Testament of a Fisherman,* which has often been published but which bears repeating here.

"I fish because I love to; because I love the environs where trout are found, which are invariably beautiful, and hate the environs where crowds of people are found, which are invariably ugly; because of all the television commercials, cocktail parties and assorted social posturing I thus escape; because in a world where most men seem to spend their lives doing things they hate, my fishing is at once an endless source of delight and an act of small rebellion; because trout do not lie or cheat and cannot be bought or bribed or impressed by power, but respond only to quietude and humility and endless patience; because I suspect that men are going along this way for the last time, and I for one don't

John Voelker with a handfull of happiness.

want to waste the trip; because mercifully, there are no telephones on trout waters; because only in the woods can I find solitude without loneliness; because bourbon out of an old tin cup always tastes better out there; because maybe one day I will catch a mermaid; and finally, not because I regard fishing as being so terribly important, but because I suspect that so many of the other concerns of men are equally unimportant—and not nearly so much fun."

This says it all, and says it well, being probably the finest expression ever of the real meaning to the life John chose above all others. Those who read this testament and still do not understand can, as I heard John remark to an industrial tycoon who questioned his lack of drive, "Go ahead with your concerns. I won't bother you if you don't bother me."

In 1963, shortly after retiring, John found one of his favorite trouting spots in Sands Township variously referred to as Uncle Tom's Pond, Fisherman's Pond or Frenchman's Pond, was actually privately owned and that the owner was dickering with a timber company for its sale. John promptly topped the asking price by $1,000 and thus acquired his own little section of the wilderness.

The pond was really an inactive beaver flowage on a small feeder stream of the East Branch of the Escanaba River. The bush road leading to it winds for several miles through typical U.P. woodlands of Norways and jack pines (some portions of which have recently been logged off) becoming rougher as it progresses. At one point it drops down over a rocky ledge; a discouragement to any berry-picking tourists who get that far. John added to the uncertainty by festooning nearby trees with various sections of defunct car anatomies: rusted, bent and perforated mufflers, hubcaps, tailpipes and oil pans.

Further along the road was blocked at an impossible-to-detour spot with a cable and lock, the combination of which was known only to a few of John's angling friends.

Another half mile, marked at intervals by small signs signifying that this was the realm of the "U.P. Cribbage Champ," and that up ahead lies the "Little Hollerdry Inn," and suddenly the glint of dark water is glimpsed through the trees. A final steep grade dropped down to a huge outcropping of Precambrian granite whereon rested John's retreat.

A tool shed, brick fireplace and grill, outdoor bar and picnic table, first-aid station (outhouse) and sundry church pews and rickety chairs decorated the small clearing. Chipmunks scurried about everywhere. Red squirrels chattered from the treetops and the occasional drumming of a grouse could be heard.

The camp building itself, shaped like a small barn, was high ceilinged with a steeply pitched roof and topped by an old school bell. The cabin was begun in April, 1966 and finished by May 4, 1966 John Pendergrath being the boss carpenter. Its interior was so full of assorted furnishings, implements and artifacts that there was just barely room for perhaps a half dozen people to sit. Empty bourbon bottles lined a high shelf on one side of the cabin. A framed portrait of a lovely, unknown lady in a state of dishabille was centered beneath. A small Franklin stove served to take the chill off or to dry wet clothes. Also prominent were dozens of ancient bottles filled with bouquets of dried forbes, flowers and grasses native to the region, a cribbage board centering a circular table and the ingredients necessary to construct John's justly famous Old Fashioneds.

An old carpet-covered ice box was securely chained to an outer wall, as John said, to protect the beer from possible bear bandits.

The pond itself averaged 50 to 75 feet in width and was at least a half mile long. On the camp side the wall of spruce and fir trees grew to within a few yards of the water's edge. On the far side, however, there was a low, boggy space of some 20 or 30 yards between the pond edge and the trees. Plank walkways spanned the bog and at intervals ran out to small docks on the edge of the pond. Most anglers have heard of Norway's great Aroy River's "Platforms of Despair." I have never fished that par-

162

ticular hallowed salmon reach but I have many times had the great pleasure of fishing from John's platforms of enchantment.

Each small dock was furnished with a milk crate or apple box. Seated there one could look down into the clear, still water where a multitude of little green spheres and filaments of elodea and algae gently rolled, while perhaps above a hatch of midges hung like smoke, rising up and down just above the surface in a measured rhythm. Bright as its brookies were it was impossible to make them out while free-swimming, even when smooth spreading rings on the surface marked rises to ascending nymphs or drifting flies.

Aquatic life in Frenchman's Pond is on a reduced scale. No Hendricksons, brown drakes or evening duns live there; only *chironomid* midges and tiny races of *Ephemera* such as the many brooded genera of *Cloen* and *Caenis* mayflies, requiring very fine tippets and wee fly imitations for any chance of success. Even the ants that occasionally fall from pondside vegetation into the water are tiny, requiring a size 18 or 20 imitation to fool the unusually wary brookies.

Access to this area was via a rainbow arched bridge near the pond's center, installed in 1967. At the crest of the bridge were three more weathered church pews, for observation and quiet contemplation. A small sign proclaimed this to be a "Chipmunk Crossing" and so it was. Another sign, hand-lettered on a shingle and posted near the camp end of the bridge, stated the house rules: "Flies only, nine-inch minimum, five fish limit."

Although he had solitude in his retreat John certainly did not suffer from loneliness. Some of his local cronies were always on hand and friends often visited many of whom, while they could afford to fish anywhere in the world, preferred Johnny's company and his lovely hideaway.

The camp on Frenchman's Pond served as headquarters and clubhouse for a host of far-flung angling friends over the years. It had an atmosphere I've never found duplicated anywhere; a spot of infinite peace and relaxation. Its solitude was unmarred, even by an occasional jet bomber passing high overhead from the not-too-distant K. I. Sawyer Air Force Base south of Marquette.

The knowledge that the quiet beaver flowage in front of you was inhabited with a host of lovely but wary brook trout somehow seemed less important, even to we avid brookie aficionados, than just being there. Sitting on the ancient pews overlooking some quarter mile of the pond, completely relaxed and listening to John's humorous anecdotes while secondarily watching for rises, life seemed full and complete.

No matter how fast or how slow the fishing action, when 4:00 p.m. came all hands present retired to the shack for the cocktail hour. John was generally the first one in and lost no time in mixing up a batch of Old Fashioned's using four-ounce shots of Cabin Still or Evan Williams Kentucky Bourbon for the keystone of each. This was always the high point of every day spent at Frenchman's Pond. As the potent drinks even further mellowed already relaxed anglers the stories assumed the scope of sagas, with John always the gruff but genial toastmaster.

In his mature years John was about six feet and 180 pounds, with gray hair and heavy sideburns. Faraway-looking eyes were set under a brow wrinkled by both years and weather. His nose was prominent and his jaw square-cut. He reminded me vaguely of John Wayne although someone else had to say that before I realized the truth of it. Like Wayne he had the primordial aspect of a self-sufficient, self-made man; rough and ready and not hesitant to call a spade a spade. Arnold Gingrich, founding editor of *Esquire* magazine and fellow fly fishing addict, once aptly described John as: "The character's character and the curmudgeon's curmudgeon."

There are few like him left that I know of and none who could ever take his place.

John's wife of many years, Grace, is a quiet, unassuming and patient lady who put up with John's barroom style piano playing, cribbage bouts, black Italian cigars and endless trouting safaris and loved him despite it all.

John and Grace had three daughters all long since grown and with offspring of their own. He had several local fishing companions. Perhaps the closest during his later years was Lloyd Anderson. Lloyd had operated a Texaco station in Negaunee for many years and was another whom I had known since my high school days. After his retirement in the early 1970s he and John fished together frequently, both averaging at least three days per week at Frenchman's Pond.

I never knew of anyone who didn't like John, even those who disagreed with him. John, on the other hand, didn't cotton to everyone. He had good friends from all walks of life, but couldn't be bothered with men who were more interested in amassing wealth than anything else and especially those who in doing so ignored all environmental concerns.

John always impressed me as a man who had his priorities in the right order. If ever there was a full life lived well it was John's. I feel proud to have known this man and to be accepted in his friendship circle. When it comes my time to pack up and head for the far shore one of the last faces I'll see in memory (and I hope one of the first to greet me at the other side) will be that of Johnny Voelker.

164

Chapter 34
Final Casts

I'm not sure who first said, "The more things change, the more they stay the same," but I don't believe in this bit of philosophy. Angling almost everywhere is not the same as it used to be and never will be again.

Protecting the right of a river to exist for the enjoyment of all is close to impossible in this age of special interest groups determined only in amassing short term profits. Every individual waterway has only a very small percentage of its users willing to stand up in protecting its integrity. Public apathy is the greatest support the despoilers have. The fresh waters we have today are all we'll ever have. If we're too unconcerned to take care of them now our future generations will have nothing better to enjoy than golf or bowling.

A world in which relatively remote streams and lakes cannot support game fish because of damaged water quality is a world that will eventually impose more costs on other species, including man.

We have developed this country with little respect for nature and the importance of virgin wilderness. First we slaughtered or subdued the original stewards of the land accomplishing much of it in the continent's heartland by eliminating their major food source, the bison. Then we systematically began a rape of the land that continues practically unabated to this day. We bare the watersheds, dam and divert the free-flowing rivers, rip up the landscape with roads and strip mines, eliminate winter game habitat with ski resorts, drain or pollute our wetlands and erode what's left with ATV's and overgrazing by domestic stock. It has left us with few old growth forests, shrinking prairie and wetlands and unclean water and air.

My generation has its place in history as the one that advanced from the horse and buggy to interplanetary spacecraft. Ashamedly, we are also the generation that has done the most to defile our environment and lay waste to its resources. We have used up or destroyed more of our habitat and its natural wealth than took place in the entire previous history of our species.

As I write this, despite the so-called environmental awakening by the younger generations, the situation worldwide continues to deteriorate. Man's gift of reasoning remains overshadowed by his self-centered view of life.

This nearly unchecked exploitation has put our civilization in danger. We're in the process of running out of clean fresh water—the one substance that supports all life. The fight over water rights in the West seriously threatens rivers in the upper Midwest. Streams are greatly diminished by excessive withdrawals, degraded habitat, rising water temperatures, reduced oxygen and concentrated pollutants. The overwhelming majority of rivers east of the Cascade Range now have salmon and steelhead populations consisting almost entirely of hatchery stock. Wild fish populations are but a fraction of their original abundance.

According to the American Fisheries Society, during the past 100 years 27 species and 13 subspecies of North American fishes have been declared extinct. This includes several races of cutthroat trout, several species of rainbow trout and many subspecies of both, as well as Michigan grayling and Aurora and Silver trouts of the East.

Of all the greedy special interest activities affecting the environment the wasteful practice of extensive clearcut logging in many of our states is perhaps the worst offender. This terribly destructive method entails gouging out thousands of miles of dirt logging roads on hundreds of thousands of acres, which are then completely denuded of forest cover.

Running off the bare gray bones of the once lovely forests, the rivers and their tributaries have suffered greatly from such activity. The waters from melting snow and spring rains, with no thick, soft, absorbent mat of forest floor held together by huge root systems to soak them up, rush down the bare, parched slopes and pour pell-mell into the streams carrying great loads of silt and debris. Resulting torrents erode the stream banks and scour the bottoms. When floods subside the silt load settles and smothers the spawn, fry and aquatic insect life. Then in the heat of summer, with no water reserves being released from the absent ground cover, the tributaries fail and the rivers slow, warm and are then further depleted of life.

Another result is the rapid accumulation of dollars by involved industrialists and their political allies at the expense of all humans and other diverse species that share our world. Do those involved care? Let me quote just one statement made by the Chairman of the Louisiana-Pacific Company, the biggest producer of redwood products, to a reporter from the Santa Rosa *Press Democrat*:

"We need everything that's out there . . . we log to infinity. Because we need it all. It's ours. It's out there, and we need it all. Now."

This same individual appeared in full-page company ads proclaiming what great guardians of the environment they all were. The basic fact that people like this can stand on such unethical principles without any real challenge from the majority of their peers is an indication of the trouble we're all in. The cumulative effects of the destructive practices outlined translates into an ever-worsening future for the environment and all forms of life that depend on it—a real tragedy of short-sighted greed and indifference.

Jobs often provide the rationale for allowing other forms of life to face extinction. A case in point was the timber industry's claim that 30,000 jobs would be lost if our remaining old growth Northwest forest (necessary for survival of the spotted owl) could not be cut. The federal Department of the Interior has conspired with that industry to override the tenets of the Endangered Species Act. They have been conspicuously silent when it comes to the western salmon and steelhead crisis, which if it continues to decline will result in the loss of more than 100,000 jobs associated with the commercial and sport fishing industries.

To me the most tragic aspect of all is the seeming determination of the human race to reach the planet's utmost capacity for supporting its particular form of life, in as short a span of time as possible. Populations are rising not on a steady ratio but on an exponential curve that populations are rising not on a steady ratio but at an accelerating rate—in an area that is forever fixed, making it ever more difficult for anyone to find and enjoy untrammeled space.

Earth's human population is presently doubling every 30 years and in the course of the lifespan of my generation will have increased from two to nine billion. Our propensity for overbreeding is truly the scariest development of so-called enlightened civilization for it can be construed to be the root cause of our other problems. Although very likely the most important issue on earth it remains the most avoided one because of close-minded religious and nationalistic beliefs. The great majority of humans don't even want to talk about it let alone contemplate doing something about it.

In my view it is within reason to envision a coming generation of men who will never know the sweet smell of pines or cedars in a forest filled with life; who will never hear the haunting calls of the northern loon or the sandhill crane and who will know only a world in which water flows through plastic pipes or concrete ditches and grass is a luxury that may not be stepped on. I believe, with Lee Wulff, that: "We're living in the latter part of the great age of sport and sportsmen. Twenty years from now we'll look back on these days and they'll look even better than 20 years ago seems now."

Specifically speaking the quality of fly fishing is more important than the quantity. The angler must have room to see, to hear, to think and to be himself. Nothing diminishes these qualities more surely than overcrowding.

As I come to the end of the fishing season each year I feel more and more thankful that I was able to experience the lifestyle that I grew up with, for it is no longer available in the way it was. The angling pleasures I had in childhood and the wild areas that enriched my youth have kept alive in my soul the spirit of romance and adventure.

Yes, I know that many regard that kind of thinking as selfish and self-centered. Yet I cannot help feeling the way I do. There are many wonderful places I have been where I don't care to go anymore. I want to remember them as they were not as they are. There seem to be a lot of places like that now.

This is not to say that it's all gone, for it isn't. There are still many quality fishing experiences to be found but as time goes on these will be ever more diminished in availability. Those of us who fight under the banners of ecology are, I feel, doomed to slowly but surely lose the battle. There is simply too much power and greed against us.

It seems to me that if humans were as superior as they profess to be, our world would never have reached the stage of disintegration that is today's reality. We may be the cleverest of our world's species but I'm afraid we lack the understanding and the honesty to stand together in solid defense of what we believe is right for all.

Hope springs eternal. So long as there remains a fair chance of encountering fish, the pleasure of fly fishing will continue to lure the keen angler. I do hope my outlook proves to be unduly pessimistic, to the extent that all who read this—the fishermen of today and tomorrow—may continue this wonderful sport through the future.